How adults help children enjoy books

The Reading Environment

AIDAN CHAMBERS

Stenhouse Publishers
York, Maine

Pembroke Publishers Limited
Markham, Ontario

Stenhouse Publishers, 226 York Street, York, Maine 03909

Library of Congress Cataloging-in-Publication Data

Chambers, Aidan.
    The reading environment: how adults help children enjoy books / Aidan Chambers
        p.   cm.
    Includes bibliographical references (p. 85) and index.
        ISBN 1-57110-029-6 (alk. paper)
        1. Reading (Elementary) 2. Children—Books and reading. 3. Classroom environment. 4. Classroom management.   I. Title
    LB1573.C4383 1996
    372.4—dc20   95-24218
                                       CIP

Published simultaneously in Canada by Pembroke Publishers Limited
538 Hood Road
Markham, Ontario L3R 3K9
ISBN 1-55138-075-7

Cover and interior design by
    Leslie Fitch
Typeset by Pre-Press Company, Inc.
Manufactured in Canada on acid-free paper
99 98 97 96 8 7 6 5 4 3 2 1

CONTENTS

ACKNOWLEDGMENTS

I first used the phrase "the reading environment" in my book *Introducing Books to Children*. Early drafts of the present text were read by teaching colleagues Irene Suter, Steve Bicknell, and Gordon Dennis, for whose advice and encouragement I am grateful. Thanks are also due to the teachers who allowed me to quote from their experiences and to Margaret Clark for her comments.

1

. . .

INTRODUCTION

All reading has to happen somewhere.

And every reader knows that *where* we read affects *how* we read: with what pleasure and willingness and concentration. Reading in bed, feeling warm and comfortable and relaxed, is different from reading on a cold railway station waiting for a train, or in the sun on a crowded beach, or in a library full of other readers, or alone in a favorite chair at ten o'clock in the morning.

But it isn't only a matter of place—of setting. It is also a matter of having the books we want, and what mood we're in, and what time we've got, and whether we're interrupted. Not to mention our general attitude to reading (whether or not it is something we enjoy for its own sake) and why, particularly, we are reading at that moment (as a work duty, or for private pleasure).

These are some of the things that influence us. They make up the social context of reading. Taken together they form what I call the reading environment. This short book describes its main features, dealing with them one by one, though in fact they are inseparable and interact with each other.

If we want to be skillful in helping other people, especially children, become willing, avid, and—most important of all—thoughtful readers, we need to know how to create a reading environment that enables them. This short book is about that. And it is intended for people who work with children and reading—teachers, librarians, parents; those who want to refresh and revise their practice, and those just starting out who may be thinking about these things for the first time.

I begin by looking at what some people call "the reading process" in order to identify the essential activities it involves. Not what goes on inside our heads—the province of reading experts—but what readers have to do to make "reading" possible.

NOTE TO THE NORTH AMERICAN EDITION

This edition of *The Reading Environment* has been revised for use by North American readers. I am grateful for editorial help and suggestions from Janet Allen, especially in Chapters 4, 12, and 13, "Book Stocks," "Book Owning," and "Star Performers," where my debt to her is considerable. A term that did present some problems was "enabling adult." In North America "enabler" has come to be associated with a person who, either implicitly or explicitly, supports another's abusive or addictive behavior. Webster's defines "enable" as "to provide with the means or opportunity." I use "enable" in this true sense of the word.

THE READING CIRCLE

Every time we read we go through a sequence of activities.

One activity leads to another. Not in a linear chain reaction, beginning at point A and continuing to distant point Z, but more like a circle in which the sequence returns to the start again, so the beginning is always its end and the end its beginning.

A diagram of the reading circle looks like this:

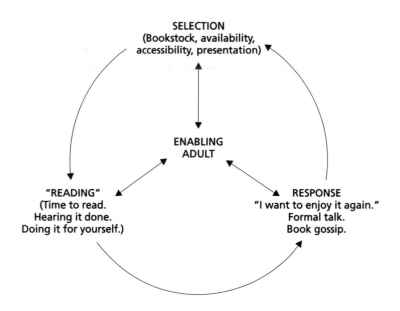

SELECTION
(Bookstock, availability, accessibility, presentation)

ENABLING ADULT

"READING"
(Time to read.
Hearing it done.
Doing it for yourself.)

RESPONSE
"I want to enjoy it again."
Formal talk.
Book gossip.

SELECTION

All reading begins with selection. Every time we read we make a choice from all the print available to us—books, magazines, newspapers, business documents, government forms, junk mail, advertisements, holiday brochures: a multitude of possibilities. This is true even when we are simply walking along the streets, which are full of "environmental print"—road signs, posters, shop-front messages, graffiti. Out of all this clutter of letterforms, we pick what we want. If we're finding the way, for example, we're mainly interested in signs that tell us where to go next.

When choosing books, we are affected by all sorts of influences. I'll be discussing some of them, the ones that relate to reading literature, in later chapters. What must be said here is that all selection depends on the availability of books. If there are only a few, the chances of finding one we want are smaller than if there are a great many. Even so, if the great many are of only one kind—only mystery stories, say, or novels about Argentina—and a kind we don't like, we are less likely to choose any than when there are fewer books but all of the kind we enjoy. So books need to be available to us if we are going to read, and the book stock must include the kind we want.

Also, however, the books must be accessible.

An anecdote by way of explanation. When I was nine, my school classroom contained about fifty storybooks. They were kept in a locked cupboard which was opened for a few minutes every Friday afternoon, when we were told to choose a book to take home for the weekend. On Monday morning we returned the books and the cupboard was locked again until the next Friday. All week the books were available, but they weren't accessible till the teacher opened the cupboard and allowed us to take one.

This may seem a persnickety distinction but, in fact, it is very important. I know of a school with a very attractive-looking and well-stocked library, but the children are discouraged by the principal from using it because they might dirty the books. The library isn't really for them; it is there as a show-place to impress visitors. The books are available, but they certainly aren't accessible. I've also been into a classroom where there were plenty of books properly displayed, but the children were only allowed to look at them when they had done well in other work. In that case accessibility was a reward used to confirm the success of some children and the failure of others. It had very little to do with encouraging everyone to read.

However, selection doesn't only depend on being able to get our hands on books. *How* they are presented affects us too. We can be put off or attracted by the way they are displayed and shelved, a subject I'll deal with in Chapter 5. All I want to say here is this. One thing confident readers know is how to set about choosing what they want. They know how to browse and how to obtain information about books they can't find. They know how to make a book stock work for them, be it a large or small public library, a bookshop, a classroom collection, or just a best friend's shelf of favorites.

Like everything else to do with reading, the way we learn best how to select confidently is to do it for ourselves, while an already confident, trusted reader is nearby to show how it is done and give help when needed.

"READING"
It is pointless to spend time selecting something to read if we never "read" what we've selected.

I've put quotes round the word "read" in order to emphasize the fact that reading doesn't just mean passing our eyes over printed words in order to decipher them. Rather, as the reading circle reminds us, the reading process comprises a number of activities of which "taking the words off the page" is only one. The trouble is that English doesn't have a word other than "reading" for the time spent looking at words on a page. And this has an unfortunate result. It often leads learning readers to believe they haven't succeeded until they are able to decipher all the printed words in a book. Whereas, of course, they are succeeding from the moment they pick up a book and pay attention to it. A preschool child who cannot yet "read," but who looks at Eric Hill's *Where's Spot?* and begins to sort out which way up it must be held, and how the pages turn, and what to do with the flaps, and enjoys all this so much she finds someone who can read the words aloud while she looks at the pictures, is being as successful at that moment in her reading life as is an academic critic busy sorting out the verbal puzzles in James Joyce's *Ulysses*.

We best help learning readers when we confirm their successes as they move round the reading circle. Going to look at a collection of books is a success. Picking out a book is a success. Deciding whether to give it more attention, or to reject it in favor of another, is a success. Settling down to "read" is a success. And so on.

Another of the most important truths about reading is that it takes time. We read some messages, like familiar signs, so quickly we're hardly aware we're doing it. Certain kinds of print, like news items in tabloid newspapers, can be read very quickly, while we're doing other things and talking at the same time. But some books, especially works of literature, may not only take a long time to read but demand concentrated attention.

Pleasure in a literary book comes from discovering the patterns of event, of character, of ideas, of image, of language woven into it. Books for very young children are designed in pictures and words that allow this discovery to take place in one reading of a few minutes' duration because for very young children a few minutes' sustained concentration is demanding. When they have enjoyed the experience a number of times they gradually learn what time and effort they must give in order to receive the return of pleasure that makes reading worth while. Margaret Meek has shown us "how texts teach what readers learn."[1] Here, we are thinking about how adults can help learning readers to concentrate on the texts that teach them the most.

This process of building up pleasurable experience, and extending the length of time we can concentrate, depends on a regular giving of oneself to books that repay the effort. So providing time to read and helping learner readers attend to rewarding books for longer and longer periods of time is an important part of an enabling adult's job.

Besides taking time, "reading" is best done in a place where the surroundings help concentration. For instance, some kinds of busy activity going on around us can be distracting. And usually it's hard to read when there's television nearby. At home we can hope to suit ourselves. But in school or playgroup or library or any other communally used space where lots of different people are engaged in many activities, it is necessary to manage things carefully so that all children have regular reading times and their concentration is protected. I discuss this in detail in Chapter 8.

RESPONSE

It is a fact of our psychological makeup that we cannot read anything without experiencing some kind of response. Literary reading affects people in all sorts of ways. In everyday talk these reactions are described as pleasure, boredom, excitement, interest, enjoyment—even using, if you're like the French critic Roland Barthes, the partly sexual word *jouissance* (joy, bliss, ecstasy) for the greatest reading pleasure of all.

Two responses are important in helping children become more thoughtful readers.

The first is that, having enjoyed a book, we want to experience the same pleasure again. This may be expressed as a desire to reread the book, or to read others by the same writer, or more books of the same kind, or simply to read for the sake of the activity itself. Thus we feel compelled to make another selection, and we start round the reading circle again.

The second response is to have enjoyed a book so much that we can't help talking about it to someone else. We want other people, especially our friends, to experience it too. We want to explore what has happened to us and sort out what the book has meant and why it is important to us.

Booktalk takes two forms. One is informal gossip, the kind of chat that goes on between friends. The other is more formal, more considered, the sort of discussion that goes on in classrooms or seminars. Both kinds of talk tend to take us back into the reading circle. We want to read what our friends have found enjoyable, and we want to reread books that seriously interest us. And both kinds of talk may have another effect. They may help change the reading circle into a spiral.

Here is what I mean. I said earlier that my main interest is in helping people become thoughtful readers. It is quite easy to find avid readers who choose books often, read every day, even talk about how much they like it. But their main enjoyment seems to come from the fact that reading, for them, is a pleasant way of passing the time. They might as well be doing something else. What they certainly do not want is to be disturbed by what they read, or challenged, or made to "sit up and think." Often they are people who only ever read in bed at night in order to put themselves to sleep.

I must confess that I'm not very interested in reading as a soporific or as a pastime hobby. Children who read at all tend to do this anyway. Reading, for me, is a means of thought. One way of saying this is that literature gives us images to think with. Or, to use David Krech's word, literature gives us images to *perfink* (perceive, feel, think) with. C. S. Lewis put it another way. When reading literature, he said, we become a thousand different people and yet remain ourselves. Richard Hoggart wrote that he valued literature "because of the way—the peculiar way—in which it explores, recreates and seeks for meanings in human experience; because it explores the diversity, complexity and strangeness of that experience."[2] In literature, he added, we look at life "with all the vulnerability, honesty, and penetration" we can command. Or we do if we read thoughtfully.

So how do people become thoughtful readers? How do they shift from being pastime consumers of print into being attentive readers of literature?

My experience as a reader and as a teacher tells me that one of the answers lies in the kind of talk people do about their reading. Some kinds of talk, because they cause us to think more carefully, more deeply about what we've read, have the effect of making us more aware of what is happening to us. And this in turn makes us more discriminating in our selection.

So we break out of a limited, flat-earth view of reading, in which we only ever read the kinds of books that are familiar to us, and discover that the reading world is not flat at all but round, with many other interesting continents on it. Even more, that we can leave the world, which itself is small, and take off, spiraling up into a galaxy of other worlds, until eventually we can roam through the entire universe of literature, stopping wherever we want and exploring whichever strange planet takes our fancy.

But we only learn how to break free, only learn how to navigate round the reading circle in the first place, if we have the help of someone who already knows how to do it.

THE ENABLING ADULT

All other obstacles in the way of learner readers can be overcome if they have the help and example of a trusted, experienced adult reader.

Any committed reader who has come from a nonreading, book-deprived background knows that, which is why I've placed an enabling adult at the center of the reading circle. Yes, all learner readers help each other too, a topic discussed in Chapter 14. The two-directional arrows in the reading circle diagram are there to remind us that enablers also learn from those they help. Nevertheless, however helpful learners are to each other, in the end they depend on knowledgeable grownups because there are some things about every craft and every art—reading is both art and craft—that you only know from experience and can only be passed on by those who've learned them by experience.

If all this makes sense, if the ideas fit with your own experience as a reader, it is time to look more closely at creating an environment that best helps readers as they travel round the reading circle.

3
. . .

THE SET AND THE SETTING

Two things influence the outcome of every human activity, helping to determine whether it is enjoyable or not, be the activity public or private, gregarious or solitary, formal or informal. Borrowing terms from the psychologists, I've called them "the set" and "the setting."

By "the set" I mean that mix of mental and emotional attitudes we bring to the things we do. Our expectations, previous experience, and knowledge, our present mood, our relationship with other participants, even the time of day and the weather: all these factors condition the way we behave while we're doing something.

By "the setting" I mean the physical surroundings, and their appropriateness or otherwise to the activity in which we're involved.

Thus a picnic can be a disaster if one dominant member of the party is set against it—is feeling bad-tempered perhaps because he is there against his wishes and generally hates picnics anyway. And no matter how determined everyone may be to have a good time, it is difficult to do more than make the cheerful best of things if the picnic is held, by some bizarre accident of circumstance, near a stinking garbage dump in pouring rain: the setting isn't favorable.

On the other hand, people who are passionately devoted to a hobby or sport will endure without complaint conditions which would be unbearable to less ardent folk. So we see extraordinary hardships cheerfully borne—indeed, apparently enjoyed—by zealous climbers on icy mountains, by earnest single-handed sailors floating alone around the world, and by fishing hobbyists who weekend after weekend sit patiently on the banks of rivers, undeterred by the foulness of the weather and the small size of their catches.

Set, it seems, is a more powerful influence than setting. But both play a part in forming our attitude to what we're doing, and also modify each other as they condition our behavior.

Reading is no different in this respect from any other activity. If we read willingly, expecting pleasure, we are likely to find enjoyment. If we are forced to read as a duty, expecting no delight, we are likely to find it a boring business. Settle down somewhere comfortable, and we can sometimes read happily for a long time. But if we don't feel comfortable and are bothered by numerous distractions, any but the most determined reader is likely to give up quite soon.

Obviously, therefore, we must remember that the set of both the teacher and the pupil towards reading will have a very strong influence on the outcome. And because setting can change a set of mind, swaying it for or against an activity, it is important to consider how each feature of the reading environment may affect the set of the people it is intended to support.

4
...

BOOK STOCKS

Before selection can be made, books must be *available*—they must be near at hand; and they must also be *accessible*—they must be easy to get at when we want them.

How do we make this possible for children?

No one, no community, ever has enough books. And it is very easy for the ones we have, especially those owned by schools, to find their way into places where they are forgotten. Even in a home like mine, which is small and houses only two of us, there are books in an attic room which I forget about and am surprised to find whenever I poke around up there.

Besides, people tend to be possessive about books, which is fine when the books belong to them personally. But sometimes books belonging to a community of people are so coveted by one group that they are lost to everyone else. In our underfunded schools and libraries, what we must aim for is the maximum availability of every volume. Ideally, everyone should be able to find out where a book is at any time, and should be able to get at the ones they want when they need them. A great deal of practical experience suggests that the best way of achieving this is by the following basic organization.

CENTRAL STOCK

Although most classroom teachers have book collections in their classrooms, the school's library media center is also a critical resource for all readers in the school. The media center or resource room can serve as a repository for both print and nonprint, literary and informational books which are not owned by any one teacher or class. They are cataloged by title, author, and subject, either in a computer or a card index. The librarian or media specialist can serve as a valuable resource for the classroom teacher in a variety of ways:

1. By casting a knowledgeable eye over the stock to see if it is well-balanced in kinds of books—picture books, illustrated stories, traditional tales, novels, poetry, short stories, as well as various categories of information books.

2. By finding and purchasing a variety of audio, audio-visual, and CD materials to support the print texts in the collection.

3. By providing classroom teachers with collections of books and support materials which supplement the individual classroom.

4. By giving talks and readings to groups of children, and by bringing other visitors, such as authors and illustrators, into the school, all of which encourages children to read for themselves with more enjoyment and discrimination.

5. By organizing and distributing information on books kept in individual classroom collections so that these books might be available to other teachers if needed.

Given the many ways in which the library media specialist can support the individual teacher's effort in creating avid readers, it is important they keep in close contact with each other.

The location of the central collection is important, for this affects its use. Better to be shelved along a main corridor, for instance, where the books can be got at whatever the time, than kept in a room used all day for teaching. And better in a large, conveniently placed entrance hall than tucked away in a room a long way from most of the children (especially from the youngest), however pleasant the room itself may be. Many schools are now being built with the media center and the central collection of books at the center of the complex with classrooms branching out from this area.

After all, the purpose of the central stock is not simply to create a neat organization. It is there to be used. The catalog system is meant to help everyone find out what books are available. The borrowing record system is there so that everyone can know where the books are. And it goes without saying that the library media center should be open at all times for browsing and reference and borrowing.

CLASSROOM COLLECTIONS

The central collection can be the source of supply for what I call "dispersed collections" in classrooms and work areas. While these books continue to be cataloged in the central stock and their borrowings recorded centrally as well, they are housed either temporarily or permanently in a single classroom. These books may be used temporarily to supplement the books the teacher has available for a specific project or be permanently kept for use throughout the year (i.e., reference and informational books). Besides using the central collection of books, most teachers manage to find ways of adding to their classroom libraries books which support whole class, small groups, and independent reading.

Whether the books are taken from the central collection or purchased as part of the classroom library, a well-balanced classroom collection consists of several categories of books.

1. Multiple copies of specific books are needed for whole class reading of specific novels. For example, many teachers read aloud a novel such as Katherine Paterson's *Bridge to Terabithia* while each student in the class follows in an individual text (shared reading). In this instance, the teacher would want a class set of this novel.

2. Multiple copies (4–6 copies) of several books which can be used by students in literature circles are needed for small-group reading.

3. Individual copies of as many varied titles as possible are needed for independent reading. These titles should include a wide range of fiction as well as poetry, myths and legends, and information books. The selection of a proportion of titles should be based on students' individual reading interests and the curricular needs.

THE LIBRARY MEDIA SPECIALIST

Such a system, in which a central collection supplies books for "dispersed collections," requires constant attention. Every school should have an adult in charge of its book stock, someone who is a reasonably efficient organizer and who believes that books should be read rather than left neatly on shelves. Just as importantly, however, the library media specialist should be someone who wants other people—teachers, parents, and children themselves—to help do the job. It has been my experience, as it is of many other teacher-librarians, that children's interest in books and reading is significantly related to their involvement in managing the book collection.

In some schools, one or more of the teachers may be chosen to plan, organize, and administer the central stock of books. Other schools might have the funds to employ a full-time media specialist. In either case, the library media specialist should be a valuable resource and ally for classroom teachers and students, serving as an extension of the classroom teacher. Most media specialists welcome teacher and student cooperation in the selection of new books for the collection and teachers welcome the information and resources that media specialists can add to the teacher's plans.

WHO CHOOSES?

The book stock from which children are expected to select is itself a selection made from everything produced by publishers (who themselves select from the huge number of manuscripts offered to them). So the people who decide what to buy for a school book stock are in a powerful position. It is their taste, their knowledge of what has been published, their opinion about what children should read that dictate the nature of a collection.

This is why, if a school's book stock is to represent the needs of the community it serves, the responsibility for selection should never lie with one person only. Teachers, parents, and children should help the media specialist select the books. While the media specialist will consult the school community, she will also use published resources which highlight those books which have won awards or have been noted because of the high interest or quality of the writing. While there are many ways to include widespread school participation in this process, the ideas which follow represent a few examples from working experience.

The media specialist can combine lists of award-winning and notable books. These can be distributed to teachers and students along with any available books which have been highlighted. These sample books can often be obtained from publishers or other libraries on an inter-library loan basis. In this way, teachers and students can help choose books they would like added to the school's central collection. Useful lists are available from many professional organizations. Here's a representative sampling:

- The Children's Book Council offers excellent lists of books recommended for content-area reading.

- "Outstanding Science Trade Books" is published each spring in *Science and Children*, a journal for members of the National Science Teachers Association.

- "Notable Children's Trade Books in the Field of Social Studies" is published each spring in *Social Education*, the journal for members of the National Council for Social Studies.

- The International Reading Association (IRA) publishes three lists annually which are extremely helpful in book selection. *The Journal of Reading* publishes the Young Adults' Choices list and *The Reading Teacher* publishes Children's Choices. *The Reading Teacher* also publishes Teachers' Choices which highlights books teachers judge to be "exceptional in curriculum use." All three of these lists offer annotations for the highlighted books.

- Awards. Each year the authors and illustrators who represent excellence in a variety of genres and categories are highlighted with literary honors. A sampling: the Caldecott and Newbery Medals, the Coretta Scott King Award, the Carnegie and Greenaway Medals, the *Boston Globe*–Horn Book Award, the ALAN Award for Young Adult books, the internationally judged Hans Christian Andersen Medal, the Laura Ingalls Wilder Award and the Lewis Carroll Shelf Award. Information about these and other awards is available from professional organizations, the American Library Association, and the Children's Book Council.

- Distributing lists of book reviews for teachers is often helpful. These reviews are usually published each month in professional education and library journals. If possible, each school should have an institutional membership so that new books are reviewed by the media specialist and teachers in a timely manner throughout the year. Committees can then be formed to choose from the books which teachers have highlighted. A sample of these review journals indicates the range of available resources: *ALAN Review*, *Booklist*, *Horn Book Magazine*, *School Library Journal*, *Voices of Youth Advocates*, and *Bulletin of the Center for Children's Books*. In addition, *Voices from the Middle*, a new journal from the National Council of Teachers of English, publishes reviews of books written by middle school students. These serve as valuable resources for student reviews of books which they would like purchased for the central collection.

- Student opinions can be gathered at all grade levels. For example, each class in a primary school discussed the books they would like to see added to their library. Then they elected a representative to a committee chaired by an older student with a teacher present to help with organization. The committee compiled a final list drawn from the class lists and limited only by the sum of money allocated by the principal from the book fund. When this was done, the committee visited a local bookshop, bought the books, and finally, after carefully preparing themselves for the occasion, presented the books to an assembly of the whole school, giving reasons for their choice and reading aloud short extracts.

- One of the most enjoyable ways for teachers and media specialists to learn about new books is through attending convention and local book displays. Individuals can make lists of books previewed at the book displays and these can then be ordered. While some school districts have district or county-level inservice days which allow teachers the opportunity to view new books from a variety of publishers, other schools also send teachers to content-area conferences such as the annual International Reading Conference or the Whole Language Umbrella.

- A middle school teacher recently asked her "graduating" sixth-grade students to choose books for the incoming sixth graders. She asked them to evaluate the books currently in the classroom and write proposals on which aspects of the collection needed to be expanded. The students felt in control of this critical aspect of selecting and making available the right books that would hook these new middle school students as readers.

These ways of involving children and teachers are useful at whole-school or classroom level and should be part of a continuing involvement throughout the year. In a school I recently visited, the media specialist had distributed "wish lists" to each classroom so that as teachers developed units, discovered books they wanted in the media center, or heard from students about more books by certain authors which they wanted, the information could immediately be forwarded to the media specialist so that funds could be found for purchase. This type of whole-school involvement in establishing a central supply of books that will support both the individual needs of readers and the needs of classroom teachers creates an exceptional working relationship that encourages students and teachers to view the library media center as an extension of their classrooms.

BOOK FUNDS

Books cost money. How much a school spends out of its budget is a good test of its commitment to reading, and especially its commitment to reading literature. As no school ever seems to have enough money or enough books to meet the student and curricular needs, every school has to look to other sources if it is to maximize its stock. These book funds do not have to come entirely from the school's budget. Many Parent Teacher Associations donate funds both for books for the central stock and for individual classrooms. These groups may also organize special fund-raising activities as well as assisting in writing appeals for, and obtaining, local and national grants.

"One of the largest media center collections I have ever seen in an elementary school has come together, in part, from the active solicitation of books as 'memory books'" says Janet Allen. "Local bookstores keep lists of titles that the school library is lacking so that when community members come to purchase books as gifts for teachers or in memory of loved ones, the library media center is assured of receiving current books needed to supplement its collection. Like the necessity of involving teachers and students in book selection, the involvement of the larger community in obtaining book funds from outside sources is an essential project. It takes a whole community to build and maintain a current collection."

5

DISPLAYS

Book displays make books prominent. They stimulate interest. They are decorative. They deeply influence the mental set of people who see them. Displays are, therefore, essential to an effective reading environment.

Putting books on show is also an important way of making recommendations by remote control. One adult can work closely with only a few children. In a large school we may never even pass the time of day with the majority. Through displays we can reach out to many more, both to those we know and those we don't.

Besides, there are times when some children don't much like us, however hard we try. Their dislike can carry over into the activities we are associated with. Then they won't read books we are seen to recommend. Displays get us out of the way. No one spends much time wondering who put them up before being attracted to whatever is on show.

Books on display speak for themselves. How well they do this depends on how well the display is presented, and how interesting the books' covers are. All in all, good displays take relatively little time and effort to set up compared with the value of their effect.

Good displays depend on two main ingredients:

- Astute selection of the books.
- An arrangement designed to attract children so that they will want to know more about the books.

The point to keep in mind is that displays work through visual appeal.

Other points to remember:

1. CHOICE OF SITE

A display set up in a dark corner of a busy corridor is not likely to receive much attention. Be sure there's room for people to stand and look without obstructing passersby. There should be plenty of light, with, if possible, some highlighting, perhaps from a small spot.

2. APPEAL

We can learn a lot from good shop-window and museum displays about such things as grouping books, the kind of materials suitable for backgrounds, the use of space, different levels and massing of shapes, how to handle display lettering and captions. Avoid anything tatty or sloppily makeshift. Think carefully about the number of books included. Clutter is ugly, and overcrowding confuses the eye.

3. INITIAL IMPACT

Every display needs one feature which has an immediate, eye-catching effect, and other features (the books preferably) which hold people's interest once caught.

But every display has a natural life span. As soon as it has become familiar, people cease to notice it. In a stable community like a school, judging when a display has reached its end is fairly easy: you simply keep an eye on how often it is looked at and how much interest it generates. Once this begins to flag, it's time to make a change.

4. MAINTENANCE

Open displays, as opposed to those behind glass or out of touching range, need frequent maintenance. Books and loose objects get displaced. Decorations get marked and damaged. Soon what began as an immaculately presented show looks tired and messy.

5. BOOK AVAILABILITY

Copies of books on display ought, if possible, to be available for borrowing or buying. Readers are impatient. When they see a book that excites them, they want it then and there. The longer the time spent obtaining a book the more likely it is that interest will fade.

Recently a teacher told me about setting up a book display in the entrance hall of the school where she had just started work, which had a very poor reading environment. Next morning, during assembly, she talked about the display and the books in it, explaining that people could write their names on a sheet of paper beside the display, together with the titles of any books they wanted to read after the display was taken down. Assembly over, the children went to their classrooms. The teacher waited behind, talking to the principal. When she left to go to her own class, she passed the display. There wasn't a book on it. Every single one had been taken within two or three minutes of the end of assembly.

This anecdote illustrates several things:

- The grabby nature of determined readers.
- The effect of a good teacher talking about books.
- The thirst for reading in ordinary children who had been deprived—and who were said by the adults who had taught them till then to be uninterested in reading.
- And an instance, by the way, of books being available (as they are in any display) but not accessible (they weren't intended for borrowing while on display).

All displays pose the dilemma of creating a demand that sometimes can't be satisfied immediately. Another element, this, in deciding the useful life span of a display. Some are set up with a life span intended to be no longer than "see-it, want-it, take-it." Others have a publicly stated embargo, such as "Nothing to be borrowed until Monday."

6. EQUIPMENT AND FITTINGS

Money is always short; commercially designed display equipment is expensive. Rather than buy costly gear, spend the money on books and be inventive in finding ways to display them. Here's a list of some of the stuff I've used:

- Units from the school custodian's maintenance ladders grouped into interesting shapes, covered with sacking and decorated with children's artwork as a background to the books.

- Packing cases used like outsize building blocks attractively covered and painted.
- Gym gear—benches, vaulting horses, climbing frames—grouped, decorated with netting.
- Art-and-craft furniture—drawing easels, woodwork benches—grouped and used as display stands.
- Tailor's dummies and stage platforms.

The possibilities are almost unlimited, and almost all of them are more surprising and eye-catching than professionally made display boards and tables.

7. THEMES AND TOPICS

There are many variations on themes for displays. Here are some of the more common:

- New books. Always popular. Everyone likes to see what's just arrived. The problem is that everyone also wants to borrow them at once.
- Books sharing some link—novels about the sea, stories about dogs, picture books that use the comic-strip mode, a number of versions of the same folktale, and so on.
- This week's author. Always popular and one of the best ways of drawing children's attention to writing they may not have tried.
- This week's artist or illustrator. As above but for deepening understanding of the visual aspects of a book.
- A selection in celebration of a topical occasion or an exploit in the news.
- Books produced by the same publisher, or in a series, or with some other shared book-production feature.
- Award-winning books. There are many children's book awards now, each of them providing an occasion for this sort of show: the Newbery and Caldecott Medals, presented by the American Library Association, the British Library Association's Carnegie and Greenaway Medals, the Lewis Carroll Shelf Award, the Laura Ingalls Wilder Award, the Hans Christian Andersen Medal, the Christopher Book Award, and the *Boston Globe*–Horn Book Awards, all annual.

- Books translated from other languages. On the whole, our children are ignorant of the literature in other languages and cultures. Focusing attention on other nationalities' books helps improve this situation.
- Books of film, TV, and radio adaptations, displayed to tie in with the local showing.
- Books reviewed by children in the school.
- Books accompanied by work done by children in response to their reading—drawings, stories, poems, models, book jackets, illustrations.
- "Our Favorites." Each class, or any group of children you care to put together, takes it in turn to select their current favorites and devise a way of displaying them. Always popular. Sometimes controversial.

8. EXHIBITIONS

So far I've been talking about small-scale, short-time displays. Now and then—say, twice a year—it's a good idea to put on a much bigger show, with many more books and elaborate backgrounds which most if not all the school can help create. Parents are invited to help and to view the books. Children's work is shown. They present a play or a poetry program or some other event. Perhaps a reasonably well-known guest gives a talk, or a traveling company of actors or musicians gives a performance. Or the exhibition is used as a focus for discussing the school's policy on reading. Most of all, the occasion is a festive time, used to refresh interest and raise awareness. Many schools are choosing a schoolwide theme with individual classrooms preparing displays related to the literature being read and the ideas being studied.

This begins to overlap with what many schools call their Book Fair or Book Week (see Chapter 12). These larger exhibitions, often brought in from outside, need careful organization. And if they are to be worth the extra work and money they cost, a special effort must be made by all members of the staff, preparing children for what is to happen and capitalizing on the event with follow-up activities when it is over.

The quality and kind of displays—or the absence of them—is another accurate indicator, I find, of the value placed on books and reading in a school. Every part of a building, in classrooms and outside them, should be examined as a possible display area. And just as with the management of the book stock itself, all kinds of people in partnership should be encouraged to arrange their own displays: teachers, teachers and children, children in various groupings, parents, parents and children, and so on. When this happens, making displays helps bind the community together as well as creating and encouraging readers.

6

READING AREAS

Human beings are territorial animals, and they are ritualists.

We like to know what may be done where, when, how, and by whom. We tend to respect places set aside for a particular purpose. And we like to know how we are meant to behave in different circumstances. So we are taught as children what kinds of behavior are appropriate for particular settings: when we are in the house of a stranger, for instance, or in a shop, or in a library, or at a baseball game, or at a birthday party. The best example of this is how all but a few people become quietly solemn when they enter any kind of religious building, even though they may be quite unreligious themselves. It seems that our minds adapt to the kind of place we are in, as soon as we recognize our surroundings.

"Reading" is like that. It is an activity that has special behavioral needs. We have to set our minds right to do it—to concentrate on the book so that we are drawn inside it and give it our attention. Experience has proved how much it helps children to do this in school if places are set aside for reading only: places many teachers call reading areas.

In classrooms, the reading area is most often a corner of the room defined by a piece of carpet and enclosed by bookshelves. (As I explain below, it is best to arrange the shelves with their backs inwards and shelves facing out into the classroom so that the books can be taken or returned without anyone having to go into the reading area. The backs of the shelves form the mini-walls of this little room-within-a-room.) Cushions, or beanbags, soft furniture of that kind, even a small armchair and an occasional table if there's space, make the area feel comfortable and inviting. There are book posters on the walls, a few books on display.

Some schools are lucky enough to have separate reading rooms as well, elaborate versions of reading corners, with space enough for displays of books you can look at and read while you're there. Because they are big enough for large groups or even a whole class, they are sometimes used for special book occasions as, for example, when a visiting author gives a talk or a storyteller or librarian does a storytelling session.

For everyday use, the rules are quite simple. You go into the reading area to read quietly and for nothing else. And you don't distract other readers by talking to them or by moving about a lot.

Perhaps it is worth emphasizing that reading areas are not libraries where book stocks are kept, for people need to talk and write and move about when they are browsing, or finding books and borrowing them, or checking references.

It was a young teacher who made this distinction clear to me. I asked him why his bookshelves were turned outwards, as I've described above, and why his reading area was only for reading and not for browsing and selecting books as well.

"When you go to the supermarket," he said, "do you cook your meal and eat it there after you've bought the food? Of course not. For my kids their library is like a supermarket. They do their book shopping there and they talk to me and their friends about what they're choosing and what's best. But they like to go somewhere else to read what they've chosen. Just like we go home to cook and eat the food we've bought."

I saw at once that he was right. It was one of those practical teaching lessons you can only learn on the job and, as I was this young teacher's inservice tutor at the time, it is also a very good example of an enabling adult learning from someone he is supposed to be teaching.

Reading areas also signify value. You don't devote a place solely to one special activity unless you believe it to be enormously important. Just by being there, used in a certain way and protected by simple, reasonable rules, a reading area announces to children, without the teacher having to say anything about it, that in this classroom, this school, this community, reading is understood to be an essential occupation.

CASE STUDY

The teaching principal of a medium-sized primary school in Oxfordshire recounts below his strategy for improving the reading environment of his school by converting a large storeroom into a reading area

> specifically designed to display fiction, to provide an environment for browsing, for smaller formal and informal book-talks, and for small reading groups. I wanted it to be a pleasant place for relaxed and enjoyable reading and discussion.
>
> At first I wasn't sure how I was going to fund this, but I had in mind that the school PTA would provide the money.
>
> I contacted our supplies department [of the local authority] and briefly recounted my intentions to the man in charge. I asked him to visit me so that we could discuss the furnishings. He brought various catalogues with him, and our advisory teacher and I met him on site.
>
> To my delight he said he felt the project was needed as the old building was under-equipped with "quiet" areas, and he agreed to fund both the furnishings and the erection of shelves and display boards. We ordered three sets of adjustable shelving which consisted of ten horizontal shelves and three oblique shelves on which to lay books for front-out display. We also ordered three low tables to furnish the room, six little cubes for children to sit on, and two upholstered benches to provide further relaxed seating. The supplies department also offered to buy three display boards.
>
> The advisory teacher and I cleared the room out, arranged for better lighting to be installed, which, after consultation, the engineers' department fitted and paid for.
>
> I felt it necessary to involve the children in the scheme and arranged with a parent to help them make two huge cushions, like bean bags.
>
> We allocated a large sum of money from the school funds for buying new books and went to a large bookseller to choose the stock.

When all was ready, after redecorating, fitting out, and setting out the books had been done—the whole project took nine months to complete—we invited a well-known author to give the first talk in the new reading area and officially open it.

(John Kitchen, headmaster, Standlake Primary School, Oxford, 1989)

This large-scale project shows what can be done if a principal and the staff of a school are determined and go about it in the right way. We often complain about how hard it is to get money for changes of this kind, yet by carefully consulting the local authority officers in charge of the relevant departments—finance, supplies, engineering—and costing the items needed, as well as being ready to do some of the hard work themselves, this school got what it wanted, mostly paid for out of the public purse.

With the advent of site-based management of schools, when principals dispense their own budgets, it should be much easier to carry out projects of this kind. Everything depends on the priorities, and determination, of principals, local administrators, and staffs.

I've often heard similar stories, if not always involving such a large-scale conversion. The key points to remember are:

1. Never assume something can't be done because "the authorities won't pay for it, or won't allow it," whoever the authorities may be. Try. Consult the people in charge of various funds about allocations for which your project might qualify. For example, curriculum development grants are sometimes available to help a school improve its book stock. Similarly, funds for multicultural improvements can be made available for buying books. Also, there may be funds available from Chapter I, ESOL, or similar targeted populations.

2. Work out beforehand, in clear straightforward language, the justification for what you want to do:

   • What is the point of making the change?
   • How will it benefit the children?
   • How will it fit into the curriculum requirements?
   • Who will do the work?

Write a short (no more than two-page) summary of your pro-
posal so that the people responsible for approving it can study
your paper at leisure. Include 3 (below) as an appendix.

3. Work out the cost of your project. Never ask for just a lump sum
   of money. When you prepare your estimate for the authorizing
   body list each item and its probable cost.

4. Be realistic when estimating, but always ask for a little more than
   you expect you'll be allowed, and know which items you'll cut
   out when asked to trim.

5. If possible, show how your project will fit in with other projects
   already in hand or in preparation. You'll be more likely to get
   your way if what you want can be seen to assist the general policy of the school.

7

. . .

BROWSING

Regular readers know the pleasure of browsing.

They know that they may find just what they are looking for, but didn't know existed, among the piles of books on a secondhand bookstall, or when scanning the public library shelves more or less at random.

People do not become committed readers on a diet of prescribed texts only, however well chosen they may be. No one can be completely successful in selecting books for someone else. We all enjoy freedom of choice, and when we have freedom, our set of mind—our attitude—tends to be optimistic and positive. We cheerfully become willing readers when following our own instincts and tastes.

Like adults, children need opportunities to find for themselves the books that will satisfy their needs and suit their maturity and personality. Browsing offers that chance.

So time to browse is an important element in a reading environment, and it brings other advantages. Familiarity, for a start. People from "non-book" homes (as I was) often feel that bookshops and large public libraries are forbidding places. All those shelves full of all those books. Where do you start? Browsing time provided in school, where there is a helpful adult already well-known to the children, and classmates to talk to about what they've read and liked, can be the way many children discover how to choose books for themselves.

Then, working with children one-to-one is important. While a group of children browse the stock, the teacher can talk to them individually, encouraging and suggesting, informally listening to what each has to say.

At the same time, while picking and sampling, children can talk to each other, discussing the books they've read, swapping opinions, and egging their friends on to read the books they've enjoyed. The teacher may have said nothing, but by providing the right setting—an attractively arranged collection of books with space to move among them—and by allowing quiet talk, the teacher has helped the children to help each other. The peer group influence (see Chapter 14) has been put to work.

HOW MUCH BROWSING TIME AND WHEN?

In a well-managed classroom, there should be time for children to browse every day. Five minutes is long enough. When special exhibitions are on display, or when the class visits the school central collection, or when they go to the local public library, a longer period is necessary. Each of these has its own useful extent of time. The more to look at and the more special the occasion, the longer the time needed. Also, of course, the more careful must be the preparation of the children for what they are to see.

I've been talking about children browsing together in groups. But of course they browse on their own too. During school time, they fit it in between other jobs, which is not difficult if book stocks are available and accessible.

What it comes down to is: there are formal and informal browsing times. During formal times children browse together, supervised by an adult. The purpose then may be to look carefully at a particular exhibition because they are studying something to do with it, or it may be simply to enjoy looking at books together as much as selecting some to read. The informal times, which may be in school hours or out of them, are when children browse on their own (though perhaps with a friend) because they want to enjoy books by themselves or because they need to find a book to read.

Unsupported by any other teaching, browsing is not enough to turn children into literate readers. The idea that all we have to do is surround children with books and everything else follows naturally is naive. Even if this were enough for some children, it certainly isn't enough for all. On the other hand, browsing is a much more important activity than its casual, apparently unstructured appearance may suggest to an inexperienced eye. In fact, regular browsing is essential.

8

READING TIME

Being a reader means reading for yourself. All reading takes time.

If these propositions are true, another truth inevitably follows. Adults who care for children as readers must make sure that children have time to read for themselves.

In trying to write this into their school days, some teachers have devised acronyms.

- DEAR: Drop Everything and Read.
- USSR: Uninterrupted Sustained Silent Reading.
- SQUIRT: Sustained Quiet Uninterrupted Independent Reading Time.

Others simply call it Reading Time.

Some years ago John Werner summarized the arguments in favor:

1. Each pupil must be given the opportunity to read, at his own speed, material of a difficulty suited to him. Some reading requires frequent practice.

2. No teacher can estimate which book will satisfy the intellectual and emotional needs of the individual. Therefore many books must be tried.

3. Such reading cannot be left to the pupil's leisure time. Many children come from homes where serious reading is simply not part of the way of life; TV, with all its advantages, has surely cut down the incentive to acquire the habit of reading seriously where this is not already part of the accepted social pattern.

4. The teacher should not always be involved in the response to a book. Emotional blocks to reading can be formed by an unsatisfactory relationship with a teacher. With classes of the size they are, it is not always possible for him to detect the problems soon enough. In any case, a previous teacher may have left him with the legacy of an unsatisfactory attitude to reading . . . .

5. A teacher cannot keep up with all the books from which a child's reading should be selected. If only directed reading is encouraged, the class will merely reflect the taste of the teacher rather than evolve their own.

6. If a child is reading only trash, then this fact should be taken into account and dealt with [at other times].

7. Many of our major authors . . . were nourished on an early diet of wide, random reading . . . .

8. The child must learn to discriminate for himself. If a pupil is allowed to accept or reject, he himself will demand higher standards in reading material far sooner than if his teacher attempts to tell him what is good and what is bad.[3]

Werner stresses what we know: that we need to read frequently and regularly during childhood and adolescence if we are to have the best chance of growing up as committed readers.

HOW OFTEN SHOULD CHILDREN READ FOR THEMSELVES?

Here is the optimum: up to the age of sixteen every child should have an undirected, independent reading time every day during school hours. Wise parents will see that their children are encouraged to read for themselves, especially during weekends and school holidays.

HOW LONG SHOULD THESE TIMES BE?

The simple answer is: as long as a child can sustain concentration and interest, plus a little longer. But naturally, the length varies according to other limits. Very young children tend to have shorter attention spans than older children. Children who have grown up in a reading family and are used to "giving themselves" to books can read for longer periods than children of the same age who come from nonreading families. Children in well-run, well-furnished classrooms can often concentrate for longer periods of time than those who are unlucky enough to be with a teacher who does not value and support independent reading (where the set is against it) or are housed in unattractive, uncomfortable rooms (where the setting doesn't help).

Nor can you expect a class of children who are not used to reading for themselves suddenly to do so just because a new teacher introduces a regular reading time. They must be prepared for it and perhaps even eased into it gradually. In these circumstances a good idea—when you have explained what is to happen and why—is to read aloud for a part of each session, because this draws everyone together and tunes their minds in to story. For the rest of the session the children read their own books for a period of time that is gradually lengthened as they get used to the activity and their reading stamina grows. Once they've become used to reading for themselves, they can get going without being read to first, and reading aloud can be given its own separate time.

A reasonable average to be aimed for is this: By age seven, at least fifteen minutes a session (with perhaps two sessions a day). By age nine, thirty minutes a session. By age thirteen, forty to forty-five minutes a session.

USSR

Of course these times are for the period of reading. They do not include settling down or preparation or the teacher giving instructions.

And they are *uninterrupted*. They are not times when the teacher checks over pupils' work with them, or hears them read aloud, or bustles about the room doing odd jobs. In fact, working on the principle that children are more willing to do what is regarded as important by adults, the teacher should be reading herself at the same time.

Sustained reading happens best if we are confident that we won't be interrupted. But also there are moments when we need someone to encourage us! One of the things a teacher can do is to provide the willpower that children sometimes lack to settle down and read. This is helped if a time is regularly set aside which everyone knows will be spent reading. A sacrosanct period is another of those rituals that condition our set of mind. Some schools do this all together at the same time. Others leave it up to class teachers to decide.

Silent? The older we get the more we tend to like to read in silence. Infant children often talk all the time they are reading. They point things out to each other, they laugh, they talk out the story, they criticize and extemporize. And they don't seem to be bothered by other children near them behaving in the same way. For them, an insistence on silence isn't necessary, might even turn them off reading. But by the age of nine children who have become willing readers quite understand that they should not interrupt other people during Reading Time and so this is a time for quiet.

I visited a class of nine-year-olds during their Reading Time the other day. Some were sitting alone at their work tables. Some were stretched out on the floor in the reading corner. A group of three boys was huddled round a table looking at a picture book and muttering about it together. There were twosomes silently reading from the same book. The room was not totally silent, but the sound was a murmur that disturbed no one. The teacher was reading a novel; every few minutes she would scan the room to check that all was well, and a couple of times in the twenty-five-minute session she walked around to see what was going on in the more obscure corners. Only once did she have to check a child who was in the opening moves of misbehaving. She did it by "giving him a look," and when that seemed not to be enough, pointed a warning finger. He thought better of his plans, and went back to his book.

This was in March. The teacher had taken over that class the previous September. Before then they had been badly taught. They had not been given time to read for themselves, had not been given most of the advantages advocated in these pages. It had taken her three months—a term—to get them used to Reading Time. But by now, three months later, they would complain, she told me, if anything interfered with their daily session.

Here is another teacher's brief note on the results of starting a regular Reading Time during a year when he was trying to improve the reading environment in his two-class village school. He took the junior class, with children aged between eight and eleven:

> Private Silent Reading periods have been a success from the start. The younger ones kept to picture books and some didn't get into them, turning pages quickly and having big piles on the tables

before them, sometimes being unwilling to share their personal store, but I hold this to be getting into the habit of using books and learning that it is an accepted social activity, surrounded as they are by books, and quiet and dedicated readers. Those able to read well became deeply involved and obviously benefited from the occasions. On the early occasions two children were in difficulties. One girl could not sustain a twenty-minute session and one boy regularly chose books he could not successfully read. Both soon adapted to the situation and have learned how to handle the period. (Howard Biggs of Childrey Primary School, Oxfordshire, March 1988)

If I were asked to name the indispensable features of the reading environment—the provisions we cannot do without if we are to enable young people to become readers—Reading Time would be one of the essential four. Two others are a well-chosen book stock and reading aloud. The fourth lies outside the scope of this book because it has to do with direct teaching rather than the reading environment. It comes under the heading "Response" in the reading circle, and is the teacher-led talk that children do together about the books they've read. I deal with this aspect in the companion publication, *Tell Me: Children, Reading, and Talk*.

It is obvious that Reading Time ranks first of these four important features. For what is the use of providing a rich stock of books if none of them is ever read? And what is the point of talking about books which few in a group know well? And though reading aloud has value in itself, in the context of helping children become readers the question must be: How much do children read for themselves as a result?

Clearly, the provision of Reading Time gives purpose to all other reading-based activities. In fact, the quality of a school can be judged by its emphasis on providing time to read and by the strength of its determination to protect that time against all other demands.

9
...

KEEPING TRACK

Forgetting is part of reading; remembering what we've forgotten is one of its pleasures.

We forget incidents, perhaps, or characters, or how the story goes. And few of us remember all the books we've ever read. For that reason, we reread the books we've enjoyed most. In rereading we recover what we enjoyed first time, and we discover details we hadn't noticed before which give us a deeper understanding, a changed view of the book.

Might it be, if we kept a simple record of the books we read, that we would increase our pleasure by making it easier to remember, as well as possible to remember more? Many great readers in the past have found it so. They accumulated their bibliography as they went along: title, author, date they finished reading. Some of them also kept notes on what they thought about the books.

During inservice courses in recent years I've come across two teachers, both near retirement age, who had kept "reading diaries" ever since they were teenagers. Each of them could open their notebooks at any page, point to an entry and immediately remember all kinds of things, not just about the book itself, but about where they were at the time, what they were doing, who they were with. Those of us who saw this happen envied them. A simple device had enriched their lives in a way the rest of us couldn't share. As a result I began keeping my own reading diary, and am very glad I did. Where reading is concerned, it is never too late.

But our reading history is much more than merely a list of books we happen to have read. It is intricately bound up with the story of how we came to think as we do, and how we came to be what we are—and what we wish we could be.

If reading doesn't affect our lives, doesn't change us or influence our behavior, it is no more than a pass-time entertainment, and hardly worth all the fuss we make of it. But if reading books affects our lives emotionally, intellectually, ethically, and in all sorts of other ways, as I believe it does, then it matters which books we put into our heads. And if it matters what we put into our heads, it also matters that we remember what those books were.

Besides, during school years, teachers have a public responsibility, placed on them by parents and the state, for what goes into children's heads. If a record of a child's reading is not kept, how can teachers or anyone else discover that child's reading history? How can you deal intelligently with a class of children if you have no means of knowing what stories, what poems, what picture books and folktales that group of children have experienced in the years before?

What used to happen when children learned to read by being drilled through the numbered sequence of books in a basal "reading scheme" was that the teacher simply kept track of the numbers. Reading was a parade-ground skill. Nowadays the best teachers do for children what literary parents have always done. They surround their children with the best literature they can find and let them read what they like of it. These books aren't numbered. Nor do all children read all the same books, whether in the same order or not.

These days, in any well-run classroom, there will be some books that everyone has read and a great many that only some have read. There will also be books no one has read yet and others perhaps only one person ever will read. In any lively literary group everyone's reading history is unique but is based on a shared experience of certain books—those the community has somehow come to regard as essential.

Consequently, it is now necessary for children to keep their own reading diaries so that they and their parents and teachers can keep track. There is nothing onerous or difficult about this. It is another simple ritual that can be taught to children as soon as they are able to read and write, and something an adult can do for them until then.

It is equally necessary that children carry their diaries with them year to year, class to class, school to school. And in order to allow for the teacher who refuses to accept the necessity or just doesn't bother, we should help children understand from the very beginning how valuable their diaries are and how important it is to keep them going no matter what their current teacher happens to think about it.

If we come across children who have never kept a diary, we should spend some time helping them catch up by recording as many books as they can remember from the missing period.

A FEW PRACTICAL POINTS

- Try to make sure reading diaries are kept in bound notebooks. Pages are too easily lost from loose-leaf diaries. The notebooks don't need to be large or contain many pages, but they should be fairly stout so as to withstand childhood wear and tear.

- Before children can write for themselves, the teacher should make diary entries as the child watches, and keep the diaries safe between times. But as soon as children are able to write and are responsible enough to look after their diaries, they should do so, the teacher looking at them once a week while chatting about the books recorded.

- Don't insist that children write comments in their reading diary, which is simply a bibliographic record, not an exercise book. Some children like to write one-word judgments such as "Great" or "Boring" or "Exciting," and there's nothing against this, but be wary of anything that turns diary keeping into a chore.

- Avoid using the diaries as a means of assessment, such as teachers or parents writing judgmental comments against entries like "This one is too easy for you" or even "Well done!" for this turns the diary into something other than an aid-to-memory, and, worse still, makes use of it against the child.

- Perhaps worst of all is when diaries are used to set one child against another in the name of competitive learning: "Jennifer has read five books in the same time it has taken you, Sarah, to read only two, and you, Charles, have read none in the last two weeks, whereas James has read six."

- If teachers are seen to keep their own reading diaries, children will keep theirs much more willingly.

10

STORYTELLING

Some people say they don't like reading stories, but I've never come across anyone who doesn't like hearing one.

Jokes, personal anecdotes, gossip (the story of our lives we tell each other in daily episodes), these are all narratives about people, telling what they did, how they did it, and why. This oral tradition goes back, the anthropologists tell us, to the earliest gathering of human beings. And out of it have grown all the forms of literature—poetry, prose stories, drama—as well as history and biography, religion and philosophy: all the ways in which we use language imaginatively to tell each other about human life and try to make sense of it.

This is true of the history of the human race and it is also true of every individual human being. In this respect, each of us lives out the history of the race in the history of our own lives.

Everyone comes to printed literature through stories told aloud. Before we can speak, people play story games with us. We call them nursery rhymes: *Hey-diddle-diddle, the cat and the fiddle. Hickory-dickory-dock, the mouse ran up the clock. This little piggy went to market, this little piggy stayed home.* And nursery tales: *Once upon a time there was a big bad wolf. Long, long ago there was a poor woman and her only son. . . And they all lived happily ever after.*

Simple words arranged in many story patterns—sounds that prepare us for what we may eventually meet in print. They accustom us to the music of language. They give us images to perfink (perceive, feel, think) with. They store in our minds a cabinet of blueprints that help us recognize the architecture of many different kinds of narrative and build stories of our own.

When we can talk, we are told stories that answer our questions about who we are and where we came from and why we are here. We hear stories about our family and stories about our tribe and stories about the world. And through these we place ourselves in time and space, and slowly construct identities that we call by our names.

If you doubt this, try playing a quite simple game with an acquaintance—someone you don't know too well. Ask each other: "Who are you?" and question each other as you answer. Particularly ask the question: "How do you know that?" You will perhaps be surprised by how difficult it is to explain who you are without telling a number of anecdotes—fragments of stories—and how often, when asked "How do you know that?" you have to reply that someone told you so—your parents or grandparents or friends or neighbors. Indeed, if you play the game long enough, you may begin to wonder if you are mainly the stories you tell about yourself. Change the stories and you change your self!

Our taste for reading literature is deeply rooted in this oral experience of story, our need for it, and our understanding of its ways and means. Nursery rhymes and tales, the traditional folk and fairy stories—including fables, myths, and legends—and the jokes and fantasies children pass on to each other: all these help form us as readers.

As I've said, it is not only young children who enjoy hearing stories; so do older children and adults. Think of that most successful form of popular entertainment, the soap opera. What is it but a televised form of fictional gossip? Think of how, when we visit friends, they like to show us the area where they live and tell us the stories associated with this building and that street, this field and that river, this person and that family. Think of the way we frequently explain everyday life to ourselves in the language of folktales: of Cinderella, and the tortoise and the hare, and Beauty and the Beast, and the goose that laid the golden egg, and Robert the Bruce learning from the spider. Think of the fictional characters who inhabit our world as if they were as real as we are: Robin Hood, Santa Claus, Cinderella, Snow White. Think of why we persist, against the evidence, in regarding pigs as greedy, foxes as cunning, bears as cuddly friends, and sheep as stupid. And think of why it is so frequently reported that people who gave up reading fiction in their early teens take it up again when they become parents and, almost as if by instinct, begin telling their children the traditional rhymes and tales.

Storytelling is indispensable in enabling people to become literary readers, no matter what their age. In fact, there is evidence to suggest that unwilling teenage readers need to hear the old stories quite as much as do learner-readers of five and six, almost as a way of making up for what they have missed before going any further as readers. Even more, they need to tell their own stories: the stories of their lives and the stories they've invented. For then they recover what they've forgotten or acquire something they were never given—a feeling for story we all need if we are to be self-sustaining readers who know how to play the reader's part in making sense of literature.

There are values storytelling shares with reading aloud, and I'll deal with those all together in the next chapter. Before that, some practical points.

1. STORYTELLING BEGINS WITH YOURSELF

Every adult has a collection of favorite yarns based on personal experience. Sharing these with children is an excellent way of establishing a good relationship with them, and then they in their turn will want to share something of themselves. And by showing not just a willingness but a desire to hear *their* stories, the adult confirms that the children's own-life stories matter, that they are as important, as interesting, as valuable as the stories made up by "authors" (the invisible people who are the professionals).

Equally important are children's own made-up stories, and they have an added quality. Life stories provide their own logic: they actually took place in a sequence of events patterned by the chronology of clock time. Made-up stories, even when they use the raw material of lived experience, present narrative problems. Characters and incidents have to be invented, the plot has to be organized, the teller has to decide between past or present tense, third-person or first-person narrative, whether the narrator is an actor in the story or an observer of it, the balance of dialogue as against reportage, and so on.

By becoming authors in this way children have to draw on their experience of story in order to solve the problem of "how to tell it." And this practicing of the art raises their level of interest in how others do it, with the result that they view story differently and they read differently—with a more conscious interest in form as well as content. They also begin to realize that readers aren't passive receivers, but are active co-makers of stories who must "fill the tell-tale gaps"—the inde-terminacies—left by the author.

Here are some examples of indeterminacies in well-known picture books:

- In Maurice Sendak's *Where the Wild Things Are,* the reader must decide where the wild things are: in Max's head while he fantasizes, or in some place "out there" to which he goes? If you prefer the first interpretation you'll find *Where the Wild Things Are* a quite different story from the one seen by a reader who prefers the second.
- In Anthony Browne's *A Walk in the Park* the reader must decide what all the incongruous items scattered through the book are doing there—Mickey Mouse looking over a wall, Father Christmas kicking a large red ball, Charlie Chaplin on the fountain, for example. What you decide will determine your understanding of the book.
- In John Burningham's *Granpa* the reader must piece together the dialogue without the help of any narrative commentary, and must decide what the empty chair near the end of the book means.

Only when we fill those gaps, and the many others like them to be found in every story no matter how simple it may seem, do we reach an understanding of what is being said and achieve a feeling of pleasure and satisfaction.

Children can do all this, learn all this, from listening to stories and telling their own, many months before they can read or write. Indeed, research suggests that on the richness of this preparatory storying will depend a child's facility and progress as a reader of print.

2. BUILD YOUR OWN COLLECTION OF FAVORITE STORIES FROM WRITTEN SOURCES
These will be of two main kinds:

- stories on which you can improvise, and
- stories that should be told exactly as they are written.

An example of the first kind is "Cinderella." Certain key incidents must be included, but there is no definitive way of telling them.

The telling can be short or long, comic or romantic, naturalistic or satiric of social attitudes, and so on. Many folk and fairy tales are like that: plot structures on which the storyteller may embroider. Some invite improvisation but contain a few traditionally hallowed passages without which the tale doesn't seem to be quite right, such as the one in "The Three Little Pigs" where the wolf says, "I'll huff and I'll puff and I'll blow your house down."

Other stories are told with such personality of style that to tell them any other way is to remove their most essential quality. Beatrix Potter's Peter Rabbit stories and Rudyard Kipling's *Just So Stories* are like that. If we don't want to read these aloud, the only way to "tell" them is to learn them by heart and repeat them exactly, like a pianist playing a score. What is left to the storyteller is the pacing of the tale, the treatment of dialogue and so on—the interpretation of the score, as it were. But then, this is also true of reading aloud. The difference is that when a story is told, the personality of the "performer" makes a stronger direct impact on the audience than it does (or should) when the story is read aloud. The two activities are not the same. Storytelling is a performer-and-audience-focused activity; reading aloud is a text-focused activity. The shift from one to the other is important and changes the nature of the listener's experience.

3. CHOOSE CAREFULLY: NOT ALL STORIES SUIT ALL STORYTELLERS

Some people can be naturally funny, others cannot. Some people are good at "doing the police in many voices," to use a phrase of T. S. Eliot's, some are comfortable only with their own voice and yet can somehow make all the characters sound different. Some people like dramatizing a tale, making it theatrical (so they are hopeless with quiet, subtly understated stories), some like the conversational fireside style (so they are hopeless at very formal stories that must be told in a "high" style).

Just as it would be tedious if we had to watch the same actor attempting every role no matter how inappropriate to his nature, so it is equally tedious for children to have to listen to one storyteller for, say, a whole school year. We should make sure that children hear stories told and read by a number of different people. This is just one reason why teachers in a school should swap classes and groups frequently for storytelling and read-aloud sessions.

4. CHOOSE CAREFULLY: NOT ALL STORIES SUIT ALL AUDIENCES

But how do you know which stories to tell? The answer is simple: by trial and error. Though, as with all crafts, it is worth asking the advice of experienced practitioners.

If you're taking on a strange group, start by asking which stories they have been told in the last few days (infants), weeks (early juniors of six to eight), months (ages above eight). Then ask which are their favorites. This is useful in two ways.

First, if one of the favorites is in your collection it does no harm to begin by telling it again.

Second, we enjoy most that which is familiar enough for us to feel comfortable and yet is unfamiliar enough to excite us with its strangeness—the suspense of surprise. Knowing the stories that are familiar to an audience helps in selecting a new story similar to those already known yet sufficiently strange to create fresh interest.

At the start of a session give the audience time to get used to you with some very short stories that also prepare them for the direction you're going to take. Then when they are warmed up, move on to the main item on the bill. The pattern might be expressed thus: "Hello, how are you today? . . . Try this for size . . . Ah, you like that, do you? Good . . . Now I've got you, here we go."

Storytelling relies on improvisation and thinking on your feet, but that doesn't mean you don't need to prepare. The performers who look the most relaxed and spontaneous are usually the ones who have prepared and rehearsed the most carefully. Confidence (on which all successful "spontaneous" performance depends) comes from knowing your material so well that you feel secure.

Everyone develops a special way of preparing but we all need to start somewhere. Here is Frances Clarke Sayers, a famous storyteller, giving advice on how to set about it:

> After you have chosen a story you long to tell, read it over and over and over, and then analyze it. What in it has appealed to you? The humour? The ingenuity of the plot? What is its mood? And when you have isolated mood and appeal, consciously, this too will color the telling of the story.
>
> Where is the climax? Make note of it in your mind, so that you can indicate to the children by pause, by quickening of the

pace, the peak of the tale. Then read it again, and over and over. Then see if you can list, or call over in your mind, the order of the events of the story, the hinges of action, in their correct sequence. With these fully in mind, read the tale again, this time for turns of phrase you may want to remember. When these have been incorporated in your story, tell it to yourself, silently, just before you go to sleep at night, or while riding a bus or subway. After all this, you will find that the story is yours forever. For though you may forget it, after years of neglect, one reading of it will restore it to you, once you have mastered it thoroughly.[4]

11

. . .

READING ALOUD

We cannot easily read for ourselves what we haven't heard said.

We learn to read by joining in with those who know how to do it, and gradually taking on all of it for ourselves. This "loaning of consciousness" by the teacher to the learner constitutes what Lev Vygotsky calls "the zone of proximal development."[5] Another way of putting it is to say that the learning reader becomes an apprentice.

Liz Waterland is a teacher of five- to seven-year-olds who thinks of reading like that. In *Read with Me* she describes how it works in practice:

> The adult first reads all the story while the child cannot read any, then the child will put in the words he or she knows while the adult reads the rest, then the child will take over the reading. All this with a known text, first of all, rather as the child learnt to speak a little at a time in forms that were familiar, until finally enough vocabulary is acquired to tackle new text (although still with an adult to help if needed). This, of course, at once negates the idea of books being "too hard" for a child or the need for any form of colour coding, since the child can behave like a reader whatever the difficulty of the text and the adult will take over whatever the child cannot manage. We do not tell toddlers "You may not try to say a word of three syllables until you can say all the words with only two." When a child tries to say "vegetable" we praise, not prevent—even if the word becomes vekble.[6]

The question being answered here is: What does the teacher do? Enabling learner readers turns out to be no different from what the skilled teacher does in every other learning activity. Jerome Bruner, an educational psychologist, summarizes it in these words:

To begin with it was she [the teacher] who controlled the focus of attention. It was she who, by slow and often dramatized presentation, demonstrated the task to be possible. She was the one with a monopoly on foresight. She kept the segments of the task on which the child worked to a size and complexity appropriate to the child's powers. She set things up in such a way that the child could *recognize* a solution and perform it later even though the child could neither do it on his own nor follow the solution when it was simply *told* to him. In this respect, she made capital out of the "zone" that exists between what people can recognize or comprehend when present before them, and what they can generate on their own—and that is the Zone of Proximal Development, or the ZPD. In general, what the tutor *did* was what the child could *not* do. For the rest, she made things such that the child could do *with* her what he plainly could not do *without* her. And as the tutoring proceeded, the child took over from her parts of the task that he was not able to do at first, but, with mastery, became consciously able to do under his own control. And she gladly handed those over.[7]

Reading aloud to children is essential in helping them become readers. And it is a mistake to suppose that reading aloud is only needed in the early stages (the period people tend to call "learning to read"). In fact it has such value, and learning to read is such a long-term process, and the bit we call "learning" such a small part of it, that *reading aloud is necessary all through the school years.*

Ideally, every child should hear a piece of literature read aloud every day. Certainly, no teacher should be regarded as competent who does not ensure that this happens with the children in her charge. She may not read aloud to them herself every day, but she makes sure that someone does.

Why is reading aloud so important? For these reasons at least:

1. LEARNING HOW IT GOES

Every time we hear a story or a poem or any other kind of writing read aloud, we acquire another example of how that kind of writing "works," how it is constructed, what to expect of it, and so on. In other words, listening to books read aloud prepares us for what we may find, and what we should look out for, as we perform the more difficult task of reading print for ourselves.

In listening to someone reading aloud, we place the burden of responsibility on her. We don't feel we must succeed with the print but that she must succeed in holding our attention by what she does with it. So we relax, we don't feel threatened, we're protected by the competence of the performer. And as we listen we become used to the Text—not the print itself (which is usually called the text), but the experience of the story or poem itself as we know it inside our heads (which I've called the Text). When the time comes to tackle print on our own, we're prepared for what we find communicated by it. We know what kind of Text is held in the language of the text. (In fact we are finally able to tackle the text ourselves *because* we know what to expect it to do to us and what we must do to it.)

This is the process of "taking it on" that Liz Waterland and Jerome Bruner describe. And it can't happen except through reading aloud. Why? For this reason:

2. DISCOVERING THE DRAMA OF PRINT

How do we learn that the marks made on paper are not just ways of representing words with dictionary meanings but are also capable of a kind of magic? If we know how, we can discover in them people who talk, events that happen, ideas we have never encountered before. They can frighten or amuse, can make us feel sad or happy, can invigorate and refresh us. No wonder nonreaders find it hard to understand what it is that readers get from print, and how they get it, and sometimes think reading—or at least literary reading—is a mystery.

The only answer is for those who know how to work the magic to show those who don't how it happens. The problem with print is that the results of bringing it alive take place inside the reader's head. They can't be taken out and displayed. The nearest we can come is to read aloud in such a way that listeners are given a sense of the drama we readers have found in a passage of print.

All writing is a kind of playscript. To enjoy a story or a poem you have to know how to convert print into the movement of action, the sound of characters thinking and talking, while giving every "scene," every sequence, the right pace (slow or fast or a silent pause) that will turn printed information into vivid drama.

We discover how to do this when listening to someone bringing print alive by reading aloud, as we observe how the signals of punctuation and the rhythm of sentence structures are used to move the story along. This means that learning listeners often need a copy of the text in front of them while they listen. Sometimes they prefer to listen first and go to the text afterwards to read it for themselves. What perhaps happens then is that they replay in their heads the memory of what they heard, and so in this way form their understanding of what successful readers do. This is one reason why so often, after hearing a story they've liked, children ask for a copy to look at.

One further point. As we listen to people reading aloud, we learn about interpretation. Different readings-aloud of the same text show clearly that what readers do is interpret. This is why repeated readings of a text are both useful and enjoyable. It is most easily done with poetry because poems tend to be short and can be repeated, differently interpreted, three or four times in one session. Indeed, it is a mark of the best literary writing in prose as well as poetry that we need to reread it before we can get the most out of it—the most understanding and the most pleasure.

Picture books are invaluable in this connection, because every picture book is in itself an interpretation of a text. The pictures not only add to the words in completing the whole story, but they are also a visual interpretation of the Text the artist "saw" in his head. This is why the picture book is the natural form of literature for beginning readers, whatever their age: the theatre of the imagination in book form, showing us how readers' minds work as they read.

3. "DIFFICULTY"

At every age, whether child or adult, we are able to listen with pleasure and understanding to language that is too difficult for us to manage in print. Reading development, like all human development, happens only if we knowingly reach out for something not quite in our grasp. Hearing what we cannot yet read for ourselves puts before us texts we may decide we want to reach for.

Quite as importantly, listening to stories puts in our possession texts we might never attain in any other way. Within our community, we are more equal as listeners than we can ever be as readers. One of the things a teacher does is to make the experience of the "too difficult" available by loaning her consciousness (see pages 48 and 49) as a reader-aloud of texts which the learners cannot yet, or may never, make their own in any other way. This in itself makes reading aloud essential.

4. STIMULATING CHOICE

Those who have tried it know that one of the best ways of encouraging children to read books they might otherwise ignore is to read extracts, or even the whole book, aloud.

Here are a few ways of arranging these occasions:

- A complete story is read at one sitting. Afterwards, nothing may be said, or a discussion may occur spontaneously, or there may be more formal talk led by the teacher. Some stories seem to provoke the need to talk about them, some have the opposite effect. The good teacher will be sensitive to this and to what the children need. The main thing is that the story be experienced and enjoyed.

- A short program of stories, poems, prose passages is compiled and read as a spoken anthology, either by one reader or by a group of readers. Between each piece there may be a brief interlude or a linking commentary or whatever else seems appropriate. This is an ideal form for open days, parents' evenings, school gatherings, and other special occasions, when groups of children can give a prepared reading performance as an entertainment.

  An example: a class of ten-year-olds became interested in the poetry of Charles Causley, who they agreed was a very autobiographical writer. They decided to prepare a program about him for their school's morning assembly. They selected about ten of his poems, each of which spoke about a significant time in his life—his childhood in "By St. Thomas Water," "Convoy" for his time in the Royal Navy during the Second World War, "Timothy Winters" and "My Mother Saw a Dancing Bear" for his work as a teacher, "I Saw a Jolly Hunter" to represent his sense of humor, "Mary Mary Magdalene" to communicate his love of his home town of Launceston in Cornwall as well as his strong sense of religion and mystery. And so on. The poems were linked with a narrative about Causley's life and character. The script—poems and commentary—was made into a book (they used a photograph album, I remember), illustrated with drawings to accompany the poems. After the performance the book was placed in the school library where it was greatly enjoyed. The assembly performance and the resulting book led many other children in the school to read Causley's poems for themselves.

- Part of a novel or long text is read in order to whet the appetite. The part chosen should have a unity of its own, so that hearing it is a satisfaction in itself, while not giving away the book's best surprises.

- A story is serialized over a few days. Ideally, there shouldn't be too long a gap between episodes. Some books lend themselves better than others to this kind of treatment.

- Short poems can be said at all sorts of times, in the breaks between work on one project and another, for example. But there should be times set aside specially for listening to poetry, even if just five or ten minutes in a day. I know teachers who have established a routine during the day for any child to put her name down to read a poem at the end of the afternoon just before everyone goes home. These children find a few minutes to rehearse their reading to avoid spoiling the poem or embarrassing themselves by fluffing it. When the time comes, each reader in turn reads her chosen poem so that the school day ends with a kind of celebration, an anthology of verse to enjoy. It takes no more than ten minutes and is an admirable practice.

- Dramatized readings. A group of people—adults or children or a mix of both—prepare a text for speaking by a number of voices, rehearse it together, and then "perform" it, perhaps with a minimal use of costumes and props, sound effects, and music to add a theatrical touch—a hat, a cloak, a suitable dress, a frying pan: whatever is appropriate to the story that helps make a strong point. Usually when dramatizing stories in this basic way, the scriptwriter will include a narrator and divide the various characters' dialogue among members of the group, some of them doubling parts if necessary. Of course, all this can be elaborated into a full-scale play.

5. BEING TOGETHER

One of the most obvious but most notable aspects of reading aloud is its socially binding effect. Those who read together feel they belong together as a community, for nothing unites more than the sharing of their imaginary experiences; and they feel together physically, for reading aloud is essentially a domestic, a family-sized activity.

Everyone who has read to young children knows this is true. Children sit close, often hugged to you. They relax and become absorbed. As they listen they enjoy the security of belonging. Afterwards they use words, phrases, ideas, characters from the story in their own conversation—linguistic reference points, personal signposts that, for those who shared the experience, say much more than others can know.

This is how cultural identity is made. Of course storytelling and reading aloud both play a part, but each does it in different ways.

6. STORYTELLING AND READING ALOUD: THE DIFFERENCES

Storytelling is much more a relationship of teller *speaking to* listener. It is more like conversation, and feels personal, as if the storyteller is giving the listener something of himself.

In reading aloud the book literally *objectifies* the experience. Now the relationship is more like two people sharing something other than themselves. Not listener and teller looking at each other, but reader and listener, side by side, looking together at something else.

In reading aloud, the communication is always through words and pictures in print, coming from the unseen, usually unknown figure of the author. This author, this person who is not present, has something to give us. It just happens that one of us is the reader. But all of us, including the reader, are receivers of the gift of the story.

Storytelling tends towards the emotionally dramatic; reading aloud tends towards the thoughtfully contemplative.

Storytelling tends towards the pleasure of entertaining diversion; reading aloud tends towards the pleasure of self-recognition.

Storytelling tends towards the hermetic, the cabal, the exclusive group, limited to the powers of those who sit together. Reading aloud tends towards the permeant, the outward-looking, the inclusive group, whose powers are expanded by the addition of those in the text—powers of language, of thought, of the other (the author) who is not there.

Storytelling is culturally confirmative; reading aloud is culturally generative.

These distinctions require another book to examine. They are noted here as points for discussion.

IN PRACTICE

Time to Hear

If storytelling demands more from the performer, reading aloud demands more from the listener.

To begin with, reading aloud is less of a conversational art, less of a direct communication between teller and listener. In written language, meaning is usually more compacted, sentences are more densely constructed than in speech.

Second, quite often words in print depend on being seen if the reader is to catch their double meaning. Sometimes the way they are set out on the page is important to their understanding. In storytelling, the performer can explain and repeat and cut and edit as he goes along, and make all this seem part of the story. The reader-aloud can't be quite so adaptable to the audience. He has an *autho*rized text to follow. Explaining and changing as he goes along may ruin it. Thus the listener needs more time to take in the meaning and to understand what is happening. Reading aloud, therefore, usually has to be *slower* in delivery than storytelling.

Time to Look

Because the source of reading aloud is a visible text, learning readers (of all ages, but young children especially) often like to look at the book as well as the reader while they listen. And often when a story has been enjoyed they want to hear it again, or read it for themselves. When planning a reading you should take these impulses into account. How can the text be shown to listeners if they want to see it? Will copies be available if they want to read it afterwards?

Time to Prepare

Never read a story to children until you've read it yourself. Why? First, if you don't know what's coming next, you might easily find yourself reading out something embarrassing or unsuitable. Second, very few people are so good at sight-reading that they can afford to be unprepared, which means more than simply reading the text silently beforehand. Language that you can speak quite easily in your head can turn out to be very tricky indeed to read aloud. So read aloud to yourself before reading to others.

Of course, careful selection of texts appropriate to your audience is essential. If you select and prepare well, you can afford to relax during the performance, giving yourself up to the words, enjoying them as much as you hope the audience will. And then you can allow the session to shape itself, because whatever happens you'll feel secure with the "script." Whether to speak or listen, allow interruptions or not, pause or go on, break off sooner than intended or continue longer—these things will sort themselves out according to the mood of the audience and the needs of the moment.

"All of this," wrote Frances Clarke Sayers in words endorsed by people with long experience of reading aloud,

> demands a great investment of time. Yet there is hardly any other investment, hardly any other area of study, that yields so potent a means of making literature live for children.[4]

12

· · ·

BOOK OWNING

Keen readers tend to be book buyers. We like to possess copies of the books that mean most to us. Owning them allows us to reread them whenever we want, helps us to remember what is in them. Seeing them on our shelves and handling them now and then gives us pleasure, for books are beautiful objects—pieces of mobile sculpture that are good to look at and have a satisfying shape and weight and texture and smell.

For over two hundred years now, since the mid-eighteenth century, educated parents have bought books for their children because they know how important book ownership is. From the 1950s on, increasing numbers of teachers have realized that making it easy for children to buy books has to be part of their job—that book buying contributes to a healthy reading environment. Why? Because in some places there are no good children's bookstores available. Because many children have parents who do not buy books themselves and are intimidated by bookstores. Because a teacher can make recommendations for book selections based on her experience as a reader of books, professional journals, and award notices. Book clubs, therefore, have become an important part of many classrooms.

SELLING BOOKS IN SCHOOL
Selling books in school achieves two purposes: students and parents begin or continue the practice of purchasing books to own and teachers and schools can enhance both their classroom and central stock of books. Bookselling is usually done through book clubs and/or book

fairs. Both of these actvities can involve the larger school and community population in both the selection and buying process.

BOOK CLUBS

While teachers may disagree on the best book club for their individual preferences, most teachers order from at least one. Many actually order from several, finding that each club has different strengths and using several provides greater variety of choice. Talking with teachers who use book clubs regularly can increase a teacher's chances of offering students the best for the money they have available. Some teachers of older students make it a practice to allow students to take turns being in charge of gathering and tabulating book orders. In this way, students are again involved not only in book selection but also in actively encouraging their classmates to buy some of the books offered each month. Students can also help by comparing prices when the same book is offered from several different companies. Although there are many commercial book clubs, most teachers order from Trumpet Club, Scholastic, and Troll. Each offers books for different age and grade levels from primary through high school with bonuses for students and teachers based on the frequency of orders.

Most teachers find that there are both advantages and disadvantages to the book club system. Although it has the advantage of being comparatively easy to run, involves little responsibility on the part of the teacher, and can be stopped at any time, teachers sometimes wish they had more control over the book selections. Since the supplier is in control of the book club brochure, selection may be limited or repetitive. Additionally, students are ordering books from a mail-order brochure without the advantage of seeing the books. This can lead to disappointment when books arrive and are not what the student hoped.

BOOK FAIRS

These are bumper occasions. Children, staff, parents, people from the neighborhood are all invited to help, and to visit, join in the special events designed to highlight books, and to buy. Mostly, they are held during Children's Book Week (usually October) or in time for Christmas or before Easter or summer holidays (to help promote reading when school is closed). Once again, careful planning pays dividends, and plenty of time and helpers are needed.

These are some of the main items to consider:

1. Time. A fair cannot be put on at a few days' notice. A decision should be made at least three months before, allowing time to collect helpers, arrange for the supply of books, prepare publicity, make displays and exhibits, and obtain special guest speakers.

The duration of the fair depends on many factors. In one afternoon and evening a small country school can do for its community what a big city high school will take at least a week to achieve. The aim should be to provide enough time for every child and parent to browse and buy. This means that during the day groups of children look round the fair and enjoy the associated attractions. Some events which work well at a book fair include author talks, storytelling sessions with community members, and theatre productions. Some students will buy for themselves, others will make lists of books they would like their parents to buy for them. In the evenings and perhaps all day Saturday the fair is open for parents and people who cannot attend at other times.

2. Place. There should be plenty of space to lay out all the books attractively and for people to move about without feeling cramped. School halls are obvious sites. If necessary, more than one room can be used, but they should be close together, easily accessible, and preferably on the ground floor. Large clear notices should indicate what is being held and where. Car parking and toilet facilities should be provided, and well signposted.

3. Book supply. There are firms who specialize in supplying school book fairs, but it is best to start by inviting your local bookseller to take part.

4. Publicity. Very important and the more the better. Teachers, children, and parents should know the details of what is going to happen at least a month beforehand, and after the first announcement there should be a gradual buildup of anticipation by the circulation of a planned program of information about events and attractions. Publicity directed at the local neighborhood should start going out three or four weeks before the fair.

Posters made by the school should be offered to local stores, banks, offices, libraries, health centers, and so on.

Final letters to parents giving dates, times, and activities should be sent ten days before the fair.

The local press, radio, and television will often take an interest, publicizing the fair, especially if you can give them a "hook"—a story about a visiting author, or about some other attention-catching aspect of the fair. Hold a "press day" just before the fair opens to allow for photographs and to show reporters around the exhibitions.

5. Layout. Plan the arrangement well in advance, so you know exactly how many books you can show. Remember that small children can't reach high shelves, and some adults find difficulty in bending to low shelves. The books can be arranged by kind, for example, or theme, or author, or at random. Whatever the plan, always try to set out the books front facing, not crammed together with only spines visible. Naturally, people will want to handle books, which means that the stock can soon become untidy. Child or adult assistants should be appointed, each one with a section to look after (and to keep an eye open for shoplifters!).

6. Sales management. Take professional advice from the supplier of the materials for the book fair about how best to hold stock of the books for display, how to record money taken, and how to make certain you have an accurate count of the unsold stock.

7. Special events. These attract people into the fair but should not completely distract them from the books. Some of the most well-tried are:

- Talks by authors, illustrators, publishers, librarians, or other specialists. These should be fixed for certain times and advertised in advance, to ensure a good audience. Fees and expenses, agreed beforehand, should be paid. (See Chapter 13.)
- Storytelling and reading aloud in a room set aside from the main exhibition. Local librarians, parents, teachers, children themselves, local people who are good at it: the performers should be as varied as possible.

- Slide and film shows related to books are always popular. But they should not run so long that people stay there all the time and never visit the books.
- Models and displays made by the children are always appreciated.
- Plays and musical performances in short programs prepared by the children or by specially invited traveling performers are popular. If these are book-related, all the better.
- Refreshments are usually thought necessary if the fair is open to outsiders and often turn out to be the most financially profitable part of the event.

8. Follow-up. At the end of the fair there is a great deal of work to be done sorting out the remaining stock and returning it, checking the inventory and cash, dismantling the displays and exhibitions and generally clearing up.

When this is over, and everyone has had time to think, a debriefing should be held with all the key helpers, discussing what happened and how the event might be improved next time. The school as a whole should also be given a chance to air their opinions and ideas, and class teachers should encourage talk among their pupils about books they bought and read as a way of consolidating and developing the effect on them as readers.

A book fair is a big occasion and ought to appear so. It should be colorfully presented and exciting to visit. As a means of encouraging book buying and reading, however, fairs are only really useful if they are held at least once every school year. Ideally, these fairs would serve as support to parents and children who are already avid book buyers. From experience, however, we know that these events are the sole access to books for many parents and children.

13

. . .

STAR PERFORMERS

Meeting authors and illustrators bridges the gap between children and books in a way that no other experience can. A little girl once asked me, "Do real people write books?" Finding the answer to that question is perhaps the main reason most people, not only children, enjoy meeting the individuals who make the books they like to read. Cold print takes on a human face. Certainly all the evidence we have—in what children tell us after the event, in increased sales and borrowings, in the writing children do for themselves, in what the publishers report—suggests that authors and illustrators are the star performers among those who enable children to become readers.

Not that the benefits are all one way. Writers and illustrators get plenty in return. They learn from their audience, who help them keep in touch with real readers. They are made to justify their work, children being uninhibited inquirers into every detail of it. And they have some fun—a day or two's relief from what can be, in fact, a lonely job.

Many schools arrange visits from writers and illustrators two or three times a year, and other special guests too, for it isn't only the originators who can play this role. Publishers, printers, booksellers, librarians, professional storytellers help children discover the variety of skills that go into making books and the variety of ways we can enjoy them.

But there are practical problems that need attention.

CHOOSING THE PERFORMER

Sometimes making a choice is easy; for example, when there is a well-known local writer, or when the district librarian offers a visit from an illustrator who is touring the area. Then the visitor is personally known beforehand to someone (yourself, the district librarian) who can assess whether this person will be successful with children. Just because a writer's books are popular or critically much admired, it doesn't mean that the writer is a successful performer. So before inviting someone unknown, it's best to try and find out tactfully what this person is like with an audience.

Most states have a council for arts and humanities which provides support for, and information about, writers available for school visits. As well as advice, they can provide lists of writers and illustrators they will support by helping with fees and traveling expenses. In addition, state and local councils for reading and English often offer lists of storytellers and other star performers they have used as conference speakers. And, as always, your local librarians and media specialists are an invaluable source of information and advice.

MAKING THE APPROACH

If you don't know a private address, make your approach to an author or illustrator via the publicity department of her or his publisher. Always include a stamped, self-addressed envelope, and provide the following details:

- Your own and/or your school's name, address, and telephone number.
- A brief outline of the reason for the invitation and what you hope the guest will do.
- The kind of event you have in mind and whether other guests will be appearing.
- The age and numbers of the children involved.
- Whether the guest's books will be on sale or not.
- A selection of dates suitable to yourself in the hope that one of them will suit the guest.
- The fee and expenses you can offer.
- The accommodation you can offer, should the visit require an overnight stay. (Not everyone, by the way, enjoys being the houseguest of a family, however much the family might like it. But if you can't afford a hotel, say so.)

In your subsequent correspondence, if not in this first letter, you'll want to establish:

- The number and length of the sessions.
- The kind of session the guest will do: give a talk to a small or large group, run a workshop, meet staff and parents, etc.
- Any special requirements of the guest.
- Whether there will be a book-signing session.
- What equipment might be needed: audio-visual aids, display boards, tables, large drawing board, etc.
- Whether helpers are needed.
- Which books the guest might especially be talking about (so that you can obtain copies beforehand and prepare the children if necessary).
- How the guest will reach the venue: clear printed directions, for arrival by car; arrangements to meet arrival by public transport.

The more efficient and businesslike you can be, the more likely you are to receive a favorable reply and to avoid calamities on the day.

And it goes without saying that visits should usually be arranged at least three months ahead. Indeed, the most successful star performers tend to be booked up at least a year in advance.

ON THE DAY

- Make sure that someone is responsible for greeting guests on arrival, seeing to their needs, and generally making them comfortable.
- Make sure any mechanical equipment being used actually works, can easily be replaced if it goes wrong, and that it is handled by someone competent.
- If there are to be formal introductions and votes of thanks, see that what is said about the guest is accurate and brief.
- Make sure everyone in the school knows of any changes to the usual routine of the day and see that the guest's sessions won't be interrupted.
- Be sensitive to a guest's needs. Sometimes in the excitement, organizers forget that guests might like a few minutes' rest

between sessions, or some refreshment, or even that they need to go to the bathroom. At other times organizers can be so protective that a guest is whisked away at the end of every session and hidden in an empty room when he or she might actually prefer to spend some time informally with the children or the staff.

MAKING THE MOST OF A VISIT

A star performer's visit ought to be the climax to a great deal of reading-based preparation, and even more reading activity should result from it.

Beforehand, children will be involved in making arrangements, in reading the visitor's books, in creating displays, in writing and illustrating their own stories for the visitor, in dramatizing scenes, in deciding on the questions they want to ask, and the like. The visit should be a stimulus, providing a real purpose and out-of-the-ordinary energy for exceptional work.

After it's over the visit should be discussed: the best moments retold, worst moments learned from for the next time. Requests for the visitor's books should be satisfied. A scrapbook of the visit might be made. Photographs and videos of the event can be shown. Successful classroom events prepared for the guest (dramatizations, for example) can be performed again for other classes or for parents, or even developed further. Anything learned about writing or drawing or storytelling or printing—whatever insights the guest brought—should be capitalized on in children's own work of the same kinds.

And don't forget to:

- Send the guest and any outside helpers a letter of thanks (something else children can help with).
- Make sure fees and expenses are paid promptly, if they cannot be paid on the day of the visit.
- Report on the event to those who can help the school again (Arts and Humanities Councils, school administrators, local librarians, local and state reading and English Councils, sponsors, PTA, and the local newspaper).

From my own experience and from the experiences of scores of teachers reported to me during inservice courses I know that two conclusions about the visits of star performers are common: that they are exhausting for the organizers (and usually everyone else as well, not least the guest), and that they are immensely worthwhile and have long-lasting effects on children's reading lives.

It is equally true, however, that those beneficial results depend greatly on careful planning, attention to detail, and the organizers putting themselves out during the event.

14

· · ·

FRIENDS AND PEERS

Several years ago, after spending a great deal of money on research, the American Booksellers Association announced the not very startling fact that far and away the commonest reason for choosing a book is that we have heard about it from our friends.

Though this information may not be of much help to commercial booksellers, it is of considerable use to the enabling adults who work with children. It tells us that time spent encouraging talk between children about books they've read pays off in helping them read more. And that if we can influence the reading of the leaders and opinion-makers among groups of children, they will pass on their enthusiasm to others.

A lot of this work is done informally, of course, when chatting with individual children out of class, and at times when we're teaching one-to-one. We mention a book and loan a copy "specially for you." We find out what a child is reading that we'd like others to know about and suggest he or she talk to this or that friend about it.

This is improvisational teaching and its success depends on knowing the children very well and knowing the books just as well so that at the right moment we can suggest the right book to the right child.

There are also more formal teacherly techniques to help children share their reading and widen the spread of their influence on each other. Here are some of them:

"HAVE YOU READ THIS?"
These are times set aside for children to tell each other about books they have read and liked so much that they want other people to read them too.

Sometimes, of course, this happens spontaneously. Sarah, for instance, mentions to her teacher that she has just finished a marvelous book; the teacher asks her there and then to tell the rest of the group about it.

Waiting on the moment isn't enough, however. Nor do such times give the child reviewer a chance to prepare. What you need to do is to build into the week's activities a set time when three or four pupils can present a book each. You should make sure they think about what they'll say beforehand, and they have a copy of their chosen book to show, and that they look for details that might help make their review more interesting—information about the author, for example, or about other similar books, or a picture of the setting.

Afterwards, the rest of the group should be encouraged to ask questions and to add their own comments, with the teacher acting as chairperson, making sure that everyone gets a chance to speak, and helping when necessary. Perhaps at the end the teacher can summarize the main things that were said, and finish by mentioning titles and authors again while showing the books in order to fix them in the children's memories. If possible, copies of the recommended books should be available for people to read.

It's easy to see how this basic plan can be varied and developed. Large groups can be split into smaller, each holding a "Have you read this?" session of its own, then reporting back to the whole group at the end, the books chosen being displayed for a day or two. One class can do it for another, or older children for younger. I've come across schools who have paired with other schools to swap audio- or video-tapes of book-panel sessions prepared specially for their partners. Others have shared their reading at one of their PTA meetings and at morning assemblies.

Some teachers extend the idea to a written version. They keep a large-size card file or loose-leaf "Have you read this?" book. Pupils are encouraged to write about a book they've very much enjoyed, so that others looking for a book to read can share it. The recommendation may be as brief as a single comment, or it may take the form of a longer, more carefully considered review. (One memorable entry said simply "This is a book Carole should read.")

As a secondary school student once told me, "When books are recommended by your own age group you tend to go for those rather than the ones a teacher has recommended." Whether this is generally true, I'm not sure. There are young readers who would say just the opposite. But with those for whom it is true, "Have you read this?" sessions are the best method by which a teacher can put peer group influences to work.

BOOK GRAFFITI BOARDS

I came across this idea in a secondary school and have since seen it used very successfully in elementary schools as well. It comes from the pleasure people take in scrawling messages on walls. All that's needed is a pin-up noticeboard in a classroom or corridor. The rule is simple. Anything can be stuck on it so long as the intention is to recommend a book. This means that the title and author must be clearly legible.

What kind of item gets stuck up? I've seen:

- book covers made by readers
- blurbs copied from book covers and decorated
- long reviews written by readers
- verses about the book
- appropriate emblems (a large black spider with *Charlotte's Web* by E. B. White written on it)
- numerous parody letters suggested by *The Jolly Postman* by Janet and Allan Ahlberg
- photographs (cut from *Radio Times*, newspapers, old magazines) of authors, of setting, of anything connected to a book
- book publicity postcards, posters, stickers, badges
- extracts from a book produced on a word processor and decorated
- child readers' own illustrations
- and, inevitably, jokes of all sorts based on books.

Once children understand the idea, their enthusiasm is such that the board is quickly filled. The problem is to let things stay up long enough to have an effect. One elementary school solved this by having a graffiti scrapbook: as soon as the board was full, the children chose the most effective items from it and stuck them into a large scrapbook. The scrapbook was kept in their library so that anyone could look at it at any time.

MAGAZINES

They may be ephemeral, like wall newspapers, or more permanent, like the school magazine; they may be audio-visual (videotaped "book programs," for example). Whatever the form, as with the graffiti board, the aim is to include book-related items that may attract readers to books mentioned, anything from reviews to jokes.

SELECTION PANELS

Every chance should be taken of involving children in selecting books for class and school libraries and for displays and exhibitions.

Making decisions about selection requires discussion, sharing of opinions, thinking out the qualities and weaknesses of different kinds of books, and, of course, a lot of reading. If the panel members represent class groups they must canvass their peers for their views, and this involves further critical talk. The whole business has a real purpose (books are actually going to be bought and read by others who will expect the choice to be justified) which gives it an importance lacking in mere classroom exercises.

All sorts of useful questions will have to be confronted: How do you judge a book? What are you looking for when selecting for other people as well as for yourself? What is a "good" book? What kind of words may help you make your thoughts clear? Are there different ways of reading? And what are they? The questions may not be phrased in those words, but they will underlie a lot of the talk that goes on, and the teacher's job is sometimes to bring them to the surface in a way that the children can understand.

DISPLAYS

It is worth mentioning display making again here to remind us of the value of the activity in encouraging the people who do it and in influencing others in their choice of reading. (See Chapter 5.)

READING CLUBS

Like all fans and connoisseurs in any field, people who are especially keen readers sometimes like to gather together. It's important that avid readers feel supported and get a chance to do more with books than in-school time allows. Obviously, what can be done depends a good deal on the age and circumstances of the children. But generally speaking, reading clubs provide occasions for storytelling and reading aloud, visits from interesting guests for talks about books of the kind that might not suit classroom groups, book-related film and video shows, discussions about how to improve the reading environment in the school and then putting ideas into action, and so on.

PUPIL ORGANIZERS

When people, no matter what their age, are involved in the organization of an activity that is regarded as important, they tend to become even more enthusiastic about it, and to influence the attitudes of others to it.

From playgroup to college, there are opportunities for all ages and abilities to help with the organization and provision of books—anything from playgroup kids helping to pack away their books from the book corner at the end of the morning to college students running their own bookshop. Assisting in the class and school library, making displays, ordering and buying stock, producing publicity for the bookshop, running a book magazine, being in charge of the graffiti board . . .

It's my experience, as I know it is other teachers', that once young people are working together as readers, the problem is not finding ways of bringing peer influence to bear but finding time and resources to satisfy the demands they make for more and more books and more and more time to read because of the enthusiasm they generate among themselves. Equally, I'm one of many who have observed with deep satisfaction the effect on the reading life of a school as these peer group activities develop.

This way of working is a very good example of the kind of teaching that is not done directly, but that puts the teacher in the role of catalyst, someone who causes things to happen—the enabler who works through others: a facilitator, a provider of resources, a guide, an administrator, a background figure. In the end, what learners do for themselves, guided by a skilled teacher-provider, is more effective than anything teachers do for learners who are not involved in helping each other.

15

HELPING TO CHOOSE

Selecting books to buy for children's collections, arranging displays, telling stories and reading aloud, encouraging children to talk to one another about books they've read, inviting authors and illustrators to meet young readers: these are the important ways adults help children choose books to read, which is why I've given them chapters of their own.

But there are other ways that are worth mentioning.

BY-THE-WAY CONVERSATION

Much can be done informally, both inside the classroom and outside, in helping individual children choose a book. These are times when you can fit the choice most closely to the pupil and when you and the pupil can most uninhibitedly share your reading—opinions and prejudices, tastes and pleasures. We listen best to other people's views when we know they respect ours. When an adult takes a genuine interest in a child's own choice of book, the child is likely to take up the adult's suggestions about what to try next.

This informal, friendly gossip about books is fundamental to our success in more formal dealings with groups of readers.

"TRY THESE"

(A version of "Have you read this?," page 67.) Once a week devote a five-, ten-, twenty-minute session to talking about a few books you'd like the children to read. Tell a little of the plot, read a passage that might whet the appetite, explain what you like and what you think are some of the attractive qualities of each book. Tell anything enticing you know about the author, or the writing of the book, or any other associated detail that may help raise interest. Be careful not to say too much, and three books are the maximum, as a general rule. This idea can be adapted to printed form. A display board, or a large loose-leaf file, or a card catalog drawer can be used to make available any kind of item that might help children choose a book: such things as author profiles taken from magazines like *Booklist* or *Book-Links*, or publishers' promotional material—anything you think will attract young readers' interest.

BOOKLISTS

Lists need not be boring columns of titles and authors; think about more inventively designed broadsheets—including illustrations, brief descriptions of the books, pictures of the covers clipped from publishers' catalogs—that can be put on display or kept in large files.

Miniature versions of the same idea can be your contribution to wall newspapers, magazines, and other such items produced by the children.

MIX AND MATCH

Gather various versions of the same book—hardback, paperback, other-language, large print, and Braille editions, taped readings, videotape dramatizations—for everyone to look at and compare covers, blurbs, illustrations, the effect of the different typographical designs, hearing the story as against reading it for yourself, the dramatized version as against the written, and so on. Even when readers claim not to like a story, exploring it in this way often overcomes their dislike and usually increases their interest in books generally and in what reading is, how we do it, and what it does to us.

In the same way, put together mini-exhibitions of all (or most) of the books by an author you want the children to get to know, such as all the picture books of Eric Carle or all the novels of Robert Cormier or all the poetry books compiled by Jack Prelutsky, along with related material and objects, and talk about them.

Or take three or four books retelling the same story, as in versions of folk and fairy tales, or various editions of the same fiction, like

Rudyard Kipling's *Just So Stories*, each differently illustrated, and let children compare them, choosing the ones they prefer.

RAISING EXPECTATIONS

All this activity raises expectations of pleasures to come from reading. We need to be sure that these expectations can be fulfilled.

I once heard a teacher telling a class that they would like Lucy Boston's *The Children of Green Knowe* because it was such a good ghost story. In children's minds, ghost stories usually mean clanking chains, horrific specters, and spine-chilling sensations. There is none of that in Lucy Boston's work; and if there are any ghosts in *The Children of Green Knowe* they are of a highly speculative kind. It was predictable that most of the children in that teacher's class would be disappointed, and the book would take the blame for not being something it was never intended to be.

Better to undersell than oversell! Express doubts, be tentative rather than assertive, warn about "boring" passages or slow starts or difficult words here and there. But all the time let your own enjoyment show.

Make it quietly plain that you expect more of them as readers than the children themselves think they can manage. Help them to take pleasure in "difficulty"—the book that is on the edge of their forward reach, the kind of story or poetry they haven't yet managed to appreciate, the writer they have never heard of before. After all, what are teachers for, if not to help us go where we cannot get to on our own?

16

RESPONSE

Reading is a provocative act; it makes things happen.

One of the most important results is wanting to read again: reread the book we've just finished, or read another. This, of course, is the "response" teachers of reading are hoping for the most. They want to see their pupils starting around the reading circle again because they know that to become a literary reader you have to read continually.

Readers themselves frequently need time to digest a book they've just finished. They want to savor the pleasure, explore their understanding of what it has said to them, share their enjoyment and their understanding with others—usually, as we've seen, with their friends (who they hope will read that book too).

Reading is a social activity. And it is at its most social when we share our reading by talking about it, in a kind of profoundly important gossip. Children should be encouraged in this, which means giving them time to chat informally together without teacherly impositions. And it means chatting with them ourselves so that they hear how we gossip—the language we use, the topics we talk about, the way we listen to others—and witness our enthusiasm for print.

But if we are to help children become thoughtful readers, informal gossip isn't enough. We must help them develop their inborn facility to question, report, compare, discriminate. Teaching of this kind is a specialist skill. You need to have studied it and thought it out, need to have become practiced yourself at the kind of responsive talk which is more structured, more consciously organized, and goes deeper than everyday gossip.

This book has been devoted to the practical business of arranging a reading environment where responsive talk—what I call booktalk—

can thrive. The skill of teaching responsive booktalk is discussed in the companion publication, entitled *Tell Me: Children, Reading, and Talk*. What needs to be said here is that our talk about books, more than anything else, enlarges and deepens us as readers.

There are other helpful forms of response that children enjoy. Here is a checklist of some of them.

"FOR THE AUTHOR"

Children make a "book about the book" and send it to the author as their part in the "literary discourse." It might contain their thoughts about what they liked and disliked or found puzzling. Pictures suggested by their reading are often included, as are some of the children's own stories and poems and other kinds of writing. When appropriate, jokes and cartoons are popular, of course, and sometimes photographs. Anything can be included that the children feel best expresses what they want to say to the author.

PAINTING AND ILLUSTRATING AND MAKING MODELS

Many children find it easier, more pleasurable, and certainly less inhibiting to respond by making a picture or a model than by writing. I remember, for example, a class of children producing a sequence of pictures, one for each of the calamities in *The Eighteenth Emergency* by Betsy Byars. And I've lost count of the number of times I've seen enormous constructions of foil-covered cardboard boxes standing in primary school entrance halls as representations of the eponymous hero of Ted Hughes's everlastingly popular *The Iron Giant*.

Some children, especially at the age of seven or thereabouts, talk more easily when they are using their hands and making things. The details we find in their paintings or models lead quite naturally to questions about the thinking behind them. This in turn draws them into talk about their reading and their understanding of the details they found in a book.

ANTHOLOGIES

Poetry is perhaps the hardest of all forms of writing to talk about. The most natural response is to ask to hear the poems read aloud again, or to copy out favorites to keep in a personal anthology. Some of the most successful and enjoyed approaches to poetry with children that

I've come across have been achieved by teachers who encourage children to keep their own personal and class anthologies. Every day some poems are read aloud to start the day or end it, or in breathing spaces between jobs. The most liked are copied into anthologies—handwritten, typed, word processed, cut out and pasted down when that is practicable—sometimes decorated or illustrated.

ACTING IT OUT

It seems instinctive in younger children to respond to stories and poems by turning them into play, acting out scenes, or inventing new ones so that the story becomes their own. Older children love to formalize this into dramatized performances, whether improvised or scripted. Adaptations for puppets, "radio" and video, the full-blown business of theatre, dramatized readings in which the text has been rewritten to suit a narrator and character voices: all these are frequently used. As an author I've sometimes been entertained by children who have adapted my books. As a teacher I know how much time and work this costs (much more than painting and model making, for example). But I've always been moved, as well as amused, by the pleasure this kind of response gives children and the amount they can learn from it about the original text, themselves, and each other.

BOOK MAKING

Becoming a writer and book producer is one of the best ways to explore the writing of other people. Children are nowadays widely encouraged to find out how a book as a physical object is made, what it is that professional writers say about writing, and to try to become both writers and book makers themselves. And making books does satisfyingly complete the circle which began by selecting something to read. There is an intricate relationship between writing and reading, both as a process and as ways into and out of a text. Both are creative, both are interpretive acts. What you discover by writing is not the same as what you discover by reading. By becoming both writer and reader you can possess it all.

17

. . .

THE ENABLING ADULT

Previous chapters have described how adults can enable children to become readers. This chapter is about enablers helping themselves.

Readers are made by readers. This is a main fact to keep in mind. A great deal depends, therefore, on how much we adults read and what we read. Inevitably and unconsciously, we will try to make other people into the kind of reader we are ourselves. We will try to interest them in the kind of books we like the most. We will lead them to think and talk about what they've read in the same way that we think and talk. And without saying anything at all, our behavior will communicate the place and importance reading holds in our own private lives. Therefore:

Know yourself as a reader. Tell yourself your reading history, write it down if this helps, and think about what it means in relation to learning readers.

I know, for instance, that I was born into a house where little reading of any kind went on but where there was a lot of storytelling—local gossip turned into dramatic or funny episodes told by my father, local folktales told by my grandfather, Aesop's stories told by my mother. I know that I didn't learn to "read" till I was nine—I remember the moment it happened—but I had an infant-school teacher who read aloud to us every day. And with hindsight I know that hearing so many stories at home and hearing so many books read aloud at school before I could read for myself, made me into the kind of reader I am now: one who hears every word in his head while he reads, as if someone is telling the story. Which means that as much as anything I enjoy the drama of narrative—the characters talking in voices of their own, the narrator telling what is happening, the pace and color of the text. I also know that it was only because a friend insisted I go to the local library with him that I found out rather late (I was twelve) that there were thousands of books for young readers and that I could have any of them I wanted. It was only because a couple of secondary school teachers talked about books as if they mattered that I learned that reading literature was more than a pastime occupation. And it was a book I found for myself when I was fifteen, *Sons and Lovers* by D. H. Lawrence, that at last showed me how literature included me, that I could find myself there, the life I knew and a life I could hope to live.

Equally, it is by keeping track of what I read that I discover my prejudices. I don't much care for historical fiction, for example; and I take particular pleasure in the formal techniques of narrative, to the extent that I am often more interested in how a story is told than I am in its content. Because I know this, I know I need the help of readers who enjoy historical fiction when I'm choosing books for a school library or classroom so that my prejudice doesn't warp the selection, and I need to listen carefully to what other people have to say about the content of a story if I'm to enjoy a fuller understanding of a text than I can manage on my own. I also know that it is never too late to become a serious reader, but that this is hard if you've no regular background of being read to or haven't many books near at hand, waiting till you're ready for them.

Most of all, I know that without enabling adults who are thoughtful readers to give you guidance, it is all but impossible to become a thoughtful literary reader yourself.

Protect your time to read. To keep fresh, and refreshed, as enablers of others, we have to continue extending ourselves—by taking a chance with authors we haven't come across before, books of a kind we aren't familiar with or have found difficult. Yet, ironically, being a teacher or librarian or parent—more so, a full-time professional as well as a parent—leaves little time to sit quietly and read with energetic concentration for long enough or regularly enough to keep up with all the reading we know we'd like to do.

I don't pretend to have the answer—at least, not while our education system is run as it is. But I do know of some possibilities that have helped other people. Before I mention them, however, I want to make a further point.

Teachers are the professional group who take care of the entire population of young people, and who are professionally responsible for helping children become readers. If they entered their profession with a well-grounded, wide knowledge of the literature published for children, and with a trained understanding of how to bring it to the young, not only would the teaching of "reading" be much more effective, but teachers would have a knowledge of books inside them to sustain them and give them something to build on during the early years of their careers.

The message to any preservice student must be: read as much as you can now, because you'll never have such a good chance again.

Besides, every child has only one go at being a child, only one go at being five, six, seven, and so on. The first class you meet can be what they are now and never again. They can't wait while you discover the books you should tell them about and show them. You need that kind of working knowledge from the first day you're with them. If your training institution isn't helping you, ask why not. And meanwhile exercise your professional responsibility as best you can, on your own and along with other students who understand how important it is. Seek help from teachers and librarians who know what you're talking about. Some of the suggestions below will help you too.

Keep in touch.   As always, everything begins with selection. When we have little time to read, it is more than ever important that we make informed choices. How can we do this best?

- Make sure you have regular access to specialist review sources. Newspaper reviews of books for the young are far too erratic and ad hoc to be much use. We need the help of well-edited journals covering books chosen from the full range of those published. This means looking regularly at such magazines as *Booklist, Horn Book,* and *The New Advocate.*

    In a number of areas, local teachers and librarians produce their own review magazines. You can usually find out about these—as about other review sources—from university schools of education, the local teacher councils, your school's library service, who often produce reviews too, or from the American Library Association, the International Reading Association, or the National Council of Teachers of English. It's worth a school's subscribing to those journals the staff find most useful for their needs.

- Handle the recent books. Reviews are useful but not enough in themselves if you're to make a properly informed judgment. The best way to do this is to read the reviews, list the books you think you most want to consider and then visit, say two or three times a year, a place where you can see the full range of recently published books.

  There are two places where you can do this: In a good bookshop, if you are lucky enough to live near one. Or, more likely, at your local or state library, where a standing collection of the last year's or even two years' publications is usually kept, as well as all the reviews.

  Any school that takes its reading life seriously will make sure that one or preferably more of its staff have time twice a year to visit such a collection and come back with information and suggestions. At the very least, this should be counted as inservice training and time very well spent.

  Of course, more frequent visits to a good public children's library are useful, though inevitably you'll be limited to whatever happens to be left unborrowed on the shelves.

Help each other.   No matter how dedicated we are, most of us need the support of other, like-minded people if we are to keep up our enthusiasm, and, just as important, if we are to go on developing as readers. Apart from the informal support we get from friends and colleagues in our day-to-day contacts, there are three main forums where this can happen:

- Staff meetings. There should be at least once-a-semester staff meetings where the reading life of the school is discussed, where new books are reviewed, and where the main aim is simply to share reading enthusiasms. Perhaps one book that has been read by everybody in time for the meeting can be discussed in detail in order to respond at our own level in the way we help our children respond at theirs.

- Reading groups. Join or help organize a group of, say, six or eight people who are interested in children's reading and who are willing to meet perhaps once every three months to share their own reading, both of books for children and of books they've read for themselves. It's a good thing if the members include keen parents as well as teachers and librarians from the area. The mix brings different perspectives to the booktalk.

- Inservice courses. One of the most useful aspects of inservice courses that deal with children's reading is the impetus they provide for the members to give more time than they usually feel they should to topping up their knowledge of books. As one teacher put it: "I tell my family, 'Hard luck, you'll have to see to yourselves this evening, I've got my course work to do' and off I go to my bedroom and read so that I'm prepared for the next meeting, and I don't feel guilty about it!"

  (That people feel guilty at all when reading literature, whether for themselves or as part of their job, is in itself interesting. The same people don't feel guilty when marking pupils' work, or preparing audio-visual aids. Why do they feel guilt about reading, and what does this say about the priorities in our education system and our society?)

  If there are no inservice courses of this kind on offer, gather support from other teachers and demand them.

Help yourself. Some private aids help keep you going as a reader on your own.

- Keep a reading diary! I discussed this in Chapter 9. It's worth mentioning again, this time to make the point that the act of keeping a diary stimulates you to keep reading. You notice any falling off and that gives you the incentive to find out why and to do something about it.

- Make a simple rule about how many children's books you'll aim to get through regularly. Set a manageable number. (I'm a very slow reader, so it isn't any use setting myself a children's novel a week besides the other books I want to read, because I won't keep it up and then I'll feel I've failed. When teaching full-time, I found I could manage one every two weeks. There were periods when I could manage more, but that rule was a discipline that saw me through the times when I wouldn't have bothered otherwise.)

What is it that enabling adults, teachers especially, do? They provide, stimulate, demonstrate, and respond.

They provide books and time to read them and an attractive environment where people want to read. They stimulate a desire to become a thoughtful reader. They demonstrate by reading aloud and by their own behavior what a "good" reader does. And they respond, and help others respond, to the individuality of everyone in the reading community they belong to.

In the afterword to *Actual Minds, Possible Worlds* Jerome Bruner writes:

> I have tried to make the case that the function of literature as art is to open us to dilemmas, to the hypothetical, to the range of possible worlds that a text can refer to. I have used the term "to subjunctivize," to render the world less fixed, less banal, more susceptible to recreation. Literature subjunctivizes, makes strange, renders the obvious less so, the unknowable less so as well, matters of value more open to reason and intuition. Literature, in this spirit, is an instrument of freedom, lightness, imagination, and yes, reason. It is our only hope against the long gray night.[7]

It is my hope that by creating a reading environment of the kind I've described we can help children discover in literature this spirit of freedom and imagination.

REFERENCES

7. Bruner, Jerome. 1986. *Actual Minds, Possible Worlds.* Cambridge, MA: Harvard University Press.

Hoggart, Richard. 1970. "Why I Value Literature." *About Literature.* Vol. 2 of *Speaking to Each Other.* London, UK: Chatto & Windus.

Hughes, Ted. 1988. *The Iron Giant: A Story in Five Nights.* Illus. Dirk Zimmer. New York: HarperCollins.

2. Krech, David. Quoted in Jerome Bruner's *Actual Minds, Possible Worlds.* Cambridge, MA: Harvard University Press.

Lewis, C. S. 1961. *An Experiment in Criticism.* Cambridge, UK: Cambridge University Press.

1. Meek, Margaret. 1988. *How Texts Teach What Readers Learn.* Stroud, UK: Thimble Press.

4. Sayers, Frances Clark. 1973. *Summoned by Books.* New York: Viking.

5. Vygotsky, Lev. Quoted in Jerome Bruner's *Actual Minds, Possible Worlds.* Cambridge, MA: Harvard University Press.

6. Waterland, Liz. 1988. *Read with Me: An Apprenticeship Approach to Reading.* Stroud, UK: Thimble Press.

3. Werner, John. 1970. *The Practice of English Teaching.* Ed. Graham Owens and Michael Marland. London, UK: Blackie.

ADDRESSES

These publications are major providers of information to teachers.

American Library Association
Booklist
Journal of Youth Services
50 East Huron Street
Chicago, IL 60611

Office of Young Adult Services
Books for the Teen Ager
New York Public Library
Fifth Avenue and 42nd Street
New York, NY 10018

Bulletin of the Center for Children's Books
P.O. Box 37005
Chicago, IL 60637

The Horn Book
The Horn Book Guide
14 Beacon Street
Boston, MA 02108

The International Reading Association
The Journal of Adolescent and Adult Literacy
The Reading Teacher
800 Barksdale Road
P.O. Box 8139
Newark, DE 19714-8139

Interracial Books for Children Bulletin
1841 Broadway
New York, NY 10023

The National Council of Teachers of English
The ALAN Review
The English Journal
Language Arts
Voices from the Middle
1111 Kenyon Road
Urbana, IL 61801

The New Advocate
Christopher Gordon Publishers
480 Washington Street
Norwood, MA 02062

The School Library Journal
P.O. Box 1978
Marion, OH 43305

INDEX